Introduction to Ethics and Human Rights

Introduction to Ethics and Human Rights

Authors

Aamna Aftab
Annilea Purser
Brianna Bedran
Divya Rohit
Erwin Kwok
Faith Grace Robes
Humna Ali
Ivan Frimpong
Janice Wong
Jason Zhou
John Christy Johnson
John Zizler
Madiha Ansari

Austin Mardon & Catherine Mardon

Copyright © 2023 by Austin Mardon

All rights reserved. This book or any portion thereof may not be reproduced or used in any manner whatsoever without the express written permission of the publisher except for the use of brief quotations in a book review or scholarly journal.

First Printing: 2023

Typeset and cover design by Clare Dalton

Public Domain images on cover:

Jusepe de Ribera- The Martyrdom of Saint Bartholomew, 1634

Claude Lorrain- The Judgment of Paris, 1645/1646

Print ISBN: 978-1-77889-053-6

eBook ISBN: 978-1-77889-054-3

Golden Meteorite Press

103 11919 82 St NW

Edmonton, AB T5B 2W3

www.goldenmeteoritepress.com

Contents

Foreword	**9**
Chapter 1: Introduction	**11**
Chapter 2: Theories of Ethics	**25**
Chapter 4: National Human Rights Institutions	**49**
Chapter 5: Human Rights and Public Administration	**61**
Chapter 8: Human Rights and the Judiciary	**97**
Chapter 9: Human Rights and the Prisons	**109**
Chapter 10: Human Rights and Economic, Social and Cultural Rights	**123**
Chapter 11: Human Rights and Environmental Protection	**137**
Afterword	**163**

Foreword

Annilea Purser

Let's begin with a question: why care about ethics or human rights? This book investigates what exactly ethics and human rights are while engaging in important discussions about how we might define these topics, in what ways they intersect, how they differentially affect certain groups of people, and how they relate to various topics like technology or the environment. Perhaps most importantly, this chapter will address the question of how human rights affect your life and why you should
care about them.

To answer this pressing inquiry, we'll first turn to a definition of concepts and historical background, as well as an overview of the essential theories of ethics. Next, we'll move to the administration and application of human rights on both national and international levels and how various mechanisms work together to protect your rights. Then, an overview of important topics – including the military, police, judiciary, and prisons – and how they relate to your rights will be turned. Following this, we'll provide an analysis of the relationship between human rights and some of the most important aspects of living in the 21st century, like your right to education or housing, the environment's relations with rights, and, of course, technology. Regardless of who you are, human rights and ethics apply to your life, and we seek to show you just how important this connection is.

Chapter 1: Introduction

Faith Grace Robes

1.0 Introduction to Ethics and Human Rights

Imagine a world where the laws of ethics and morality do not exist. Without guidelines defining right from wrong leads to a dark world of distrust and lack of civilization. Humanity would perish. A glimpse of this dystopian world would include people not being able to make plans, not leaving their belongings behind them, and not trusting anything or anyone. Humans would isolate themselves from each other and live independently, fending for only themselves. People would lose their sense of self-worth and purpose in life, only feeding off the negative energy they exist within. Eventually, without ethics, the human race would decline and go extinct in just a matter of years. Thankfully, humans have been given enough intelligence to understand that having a sense of morality and human rights is an essential requirement of life. It is part of the innate human nature to have a moral sense. Humans' biological makeup determines the presence of three essential conditions for ethical behaviour including the ability to anticipate the consequences of their actions; the ability to make value judgements; and the ability to choose between alternative courses of action (Ayala, 2010). This is what makes humans human: mortality. While it may seem like ethics is a self-explanatory concept that all humans possess, there are times when the boundary between right and wrong is blurred. This is why ethical fundamentals and guidelines are established to ensure balance and the preservation of human rights.

Ethics is a set of moral principles: a theory or system of moral values. They are a set of principles of conduct governing an individual or group (Merriam-Webster, n.d.). Human rights are rights regarded as belonging fundamentally to all persons (Merriam-Webster, n.d.). While these words are defined by Merriam-Webster, there are more specific meanings and niche definitions that will be further elaborated on later in this chapter.

2.0 Ethics

The word "ethics" comes from the Greek word, ethos, meaning character, and front the Latin word, mores, meaning customs. Therefore, ethics defines how an individual chooses to interact with others (Cornell Law School, n.d.). The laws of ethics span all aspects of life. When most people think of ethics they primarily associate it with a fundamental method of distinguishing right from wrong. The Golden Rule: "do unto others as you would have them do unto you" pops up in mind for most people. For others, religious doctrines like the Ten Commandments or teachings from wise prophets come to mind. These are common ways in which people recall and retain ethical beliefs.

While most societies have legal rules that govern one's behaviour, ethical norms are usually broader and more informal than legislative laws. Most societies use laws to enforce nationally accepted ethical standards, ethics and law are not the same. Something can be deemed legal in the eyes of legalities but may be unethical in the eyes of many, and vice versa. Ethics span many different disciplines, institutions, and professions. These fundamental standards are essential to establish because ethics is what guides us to building trust, promoting fairness, ensuring accountability, encouraging good behaviour, and fostering personal growth. It prevents the fabrication and false interpretation of data to promote the truth and minimize errors. In other professions, ethics promotes values essential to collaboration including accountability, respect, responsibility, and fairness (Resnik, 2020). Following ethical principles and values, creates a better world for current inhabitants and future generations to come.

3.0 Human Rights

Human rights are defined in the name itself, the right to be human. Human rights are basic rights that belong to all human beings simply because they are human. These rights are essential to ensure the protection of all people regardless of race, sex, gender, physical and mental disabilities, and socioeconomic differences. This is especially important for people facing abuse, neglect, and isolation. These rights empower individuals to have a voice and speak up to challenge maltreatment from others and public authorities.

According to the United Nations, there are 30 Basic Human Rights that everyone is entitled to universally. The Universal Declaration of Human Rights (UDHR) includes the right to life and liberty, freedom from slavery and torture, freedom of opinion and expression, the right to work and education, the right to equality and dignity, and to live free from all forms of discrimination (United Nations, 2018; Human Rights Commission, n.d.). The UDHR was created in 1948 in Paris to ensure that all humans are treated with dignity and respect. They also protect individuals from physical, emotional, and psychological abuse and exploitation. Having human rights, enables people to freely express their opinions and beliefs without fearing censorship or retaliation. The UDHR ensures that everyone is entitled to equal treatment under the law regardless of race, sex, gender, socioeconomic status, etc. Thereby, promoting peace and stability through the fostering of respect for diversity, promotion of tolerance and understanding, and encouragement of cooperation and collaboration. Through human rights, there can be a more just and equitable society for everyone.

4.0 The History of Ethics

Ethics has been a subject of study since ancient times. Since the development of human civilizations, ethics have been practised and preached throughout millenniums. A brief history of the development of ethical thought includes ancient Greece, Stoicism and Epicureanism, Judeo-Christian ethics, Enlightenment ethics, and modern ethics (20th century) (MacIntyre, 2002).

4.1 Ancient Greek Ethics

As mentioned before, ethics is derived from the ancient Greek word, ethos, meaning character (Cornell Law School, n.d.). The earliest known ethical philosophers were the ancient Greeks including Socrates, Plato, and Aristotle over 2000 years ago. These great philosophers explored questions about the nature of morality and focus on the good life. Greek ethics emphasized the importance of living a good life, which was seen as the ultimate goal of human existence. The good life was not simply a matter of pleasure or happiness, but also involved the cultivation of virtues such as wisdom, courage, and justice (MacIntyre, 2002). Greek ethics was also characterized by virtue ethics, which focused on the development of moral character. Virtue was seen as a habit or disposition that enabled a person to act in a morally good way. The four cardinal virtues were wisdom, courage, justice, and temperance. These virtues were not seen as fixed or innate qualities, but rather as habits that could be developed through practice and repetition (Husthouse & Pettigrove, 2022).

Greek philosophers focused on the importance of moral reasoning and reflection. For example, Socrates believed in the power of rational inquiry to arrive at ethical truths. He believed that moral reasoning involved a process of questioning and dialogue. This method would allow individuals to question their interlocutors to help them clarify their beliefs and arrive at a deeper understanding of moral issues. On the other hand, Plato emphasized the role of reason and logic in ethical decision-making. He believed that ethical principles should guide the organization of society and the selection of leaders regarding ethics and politics (MacIntyre, 2002).

4.2 Stoicism and Epicureanism

During the Hellenistic period in 300 BCE, two philosophical schools - Stoicism and Epicureanism - emerged from Ancient Greece and Rome. Stoics believed in living in harmony with nature and the natural order, while Epicureans believed that the pursuit of pleasure was the highest good. Stoicism was founded by the philosopher Zeno of Citium in Athens around 300 BCE. For Stoics, the highest good is to live a life of virtue. Virtue involves cultivating qualities such as wisdom, courage, justice, and self-control. Stoics believe that individuals should strive to have complete control over their emotions. They believe that emotions are within one's control and that it is possible to achieve a state of inner tranquillity and calm by mastering emotions. Stoics also believe that people should accept the natural order of things like fate and the events of life that are outside of their control. They believe that individuals should focus on what they can control and accept what they cannot control (Pigliucci, n.d.).

Epicureanism was founded by the philosopher Epicurus in Athens around 341–270 BCE. Epicureans believe that pleasure is the highest form of good. Their version of pleasure is not seen as simply physical or a form of indulgence, but as a state of inner peace and tranquillity. Epicureans believed that the key to achieving pleasure is by eliminating fear and pain, which involves living a simple life and avoiding excess materialism. They also believed that people should aim to be liberated from external control including social and political pressures, but instead place a high value on friendship as a key to happiness and fulfilment (Diano, n.d.). Stoicism focuses more on living a life of virtue and inner tranquility, while Epicureanism focuses on living a life of pleasure without fear and pain.

4.3 Judeo-Christian Ethics

Judeo-Christian ethics emerged in the Middle East with the monotheistic religions of Judaism, Christianity, and Islam. These ethical systems emphasized the importance of faith, obedience to God, and moral behaviour. The key features of Judeo-Christian ethics include having God as the source of moral authority.

Ethical principles are derived from God's teachings and commandments as revealed in religious texts such as Moses or Musa's Ten Commandments from the Bible or Qur'an, respectively. Judeo-Christian ethics also focus on the value of human life. Human life is considered to be sacred and valuable, as human beings are created in the image of God. As a result, ethical principles often emphasize the importance of protecting and preserving human life. In addition, love and compassion towards others using empathy and kindness is an essential feature in Judeo-Christian ethics. For example, the Bible writes how Jesus commands us to "love each other as I have loved you" (New International Version, 2011, John 15:12) Christians, for example, are called to love their neighbours as themselves and to treat others with kindness and empathy. Justice and righteousness are also emphasized in Judeo-Christian ethics. In Biblical teachings, God is portrayed as a just and righteous judge who punishes wrongdoers and rewards those who do good. This version of ethics often stresses the importance of personal responsibility and accountability. Individuals are called to take responsibility for their actions and to strive to live virtuous lives (Silk, 1984). Overall, Judeo-Christian ethics is characterized by a belief in God as the ultimate source of moral authority, the value of human life, the importance of love and compassion, justice and righteousness, and personal responsibility. These principles have had a significant impact on Western ethics and continue to be a major influence on ethical thought and behaviour today.

4.4 Enlightenment Ethics

During the Enlightenment period in Europe from 1685 to 1815, philosophers such as Immanuel Kant and Jeremy Bentham developed new ethical theories. Kant believed in the importance of duty and the categorical imperative, while Bentham proposed utilitarianism, the idea that the goal of morality is to maximize happiness for the greatest number of people.

The Enlightenment period points towards an era in ethics where the questioning of religion and the rise of secularism in society. The period was a time of great intellectual and cultural change, marked by a focus on reason, individualism, and the pursuit of knowledge. Many philosophers began doubting the rationality of religion specifically, Christianity, in Christian-dominated nations like England. One philosopher and physician, John Locke, was titled the "father of liberalism" due to his highly influential published work regarding Enlightenment thinking. In one of his famous theses, On the Reasonableness of Christianity (1695), Locke establishes the teachings and compatibility of Christianity in individual thinking. Locke influenced and inspired many other great philosophers to explore freethinking and individualism.

Enlightenment ethics focuses on reason, individualism, human rights, progress, universal morality, and tolerance. Enlightenment thinkers believed that morality should be based on reason rather than tradition or religious authority. They believed that individuals should use reasoning to determine whether something is right or wrong– people used reason as the basis of morality. People of the enlightenment era also emphasized the importance of individual rights and freedoms. They believed that all people were entitled to certain basic rights, such as the right to life, liberty, and property. This emphasis on individualism was a rejection of the feudal system and the idea that individuals were bound by their social status. In addition, progress and improvement were also the main focus of enlightenment thinkers. They believed that through reason and scientific inquiry, human beings could achieve a better society and a better life. They were optimistic about the potential for human progress and saw morality as a key part of this progress (Bristow, 2017). Moreover, people focused on universal morality– the idea of universal morality that applied to all people, regardless of cultural or religious background. Many believed that all people had the capacity for reason and could arrive at moral principles that applied to everyone. Finally, enlightenment thinkers highlighted the importance of tolerance and pluralism. They believed that people of different religions and cultures could live together peacefully and that diversity was a strength rather than a weakness (Den Uyl et al., 2021).

Many of these ethical ideologies established during the Enlightenment era are still practised today in twenty-first-century Western society. One of the many modern-day examples of ethical practice adapted from the Enlightenment period includes the importance of tolerance and pluralism through the unity and harmony of different cultures and religions living peacefully in the same neighbourhood. The values of enlightenment ethics are reflected and further elaborated in modern ethics.

4.5 Modern Ethics

In the 20th century, many new ethical theories emerged, including virtue ethics, care ethics, and feminist ethics. These theories focus on the role of personal values, emotions, and relationships in ethical decision-making. Modern ethical theories emphasize the importance of reason and individual autonomy in ethical decision-making. Rationality is seen as the basis for ethical thought, and individuals are seen as responsible agents who are capable of making their own moral choices. Moreover, two major ethical approaches that have emerged in modern ethics are consequentialism and deontology. Consequentialism focuses on the consequences of actions, to maximize good outcomes and minimize harm. Deontology, on the other hand, emphasizes moral rules and duties that must be followed, regardless of the consequences (Alexander & Moore, 2020).

Another important approach in modern ethics is virtue ethics, which emphasizes the importance of developing virtuous character traits, such as honesty, courage, and compassion. Virtue ethics see ethical behaviour as stemming from a person's character, rather than from rules or consequences (Hursthouse & Pettigrove, 2003). Modern ethics also includes a wide range of applied ethical fields, such as bioethics, environmental ethics, and business ethics. These fields apply ethical principles to specific contexts and issues, such as medical decision-making, environmental sustainability, and corporate responsibility. Modern ethics also acknowledges the diversity of ethical views and the relativity of moral values to different cultures and contexts. Pluralism and relativism recognize that there is no single, objective standard of morality and that different ethical approaches may be valid in different contexts (Baghramian & Carter, 2020). These principles continue to shape ethical ideas and behaviour in a variety of fields and individual thought.

5.0 The History of Human Rights

The concept of human rights has a long and complex history that spans cultures and civilizations. Some key historical developments in the history of human rights span from an ancient civilization, religious traditions, enlightenment and revolutions, international treaties, and contemporary human rights issues.

Firstly, The idea that individuals have inherent rights that should be protected by law can be traced back to ancient civilizations such as Greece and Rome. For example, the Athenian statesman Pericles spoke of the importance of protecting the rights of citizens, and the Roman jurist Cicero argued that there were natural laws that applied to all people (Lewis, 2023; Britannica, 2013). It was not solely the works of ancient Greece and Rome that cultivated human rights thousands of years ago, but many religions value traditions that highlight the importance of preserving human rights. Many religious traditions emphasized the significance of human dignity and rights. For instance, in the Judeo-Christian tradition, the idea of humans being made in the image of God has been interpreted as implying that humans have inherent worth and dignity. Another example includes the religion of Islam wherein Islamic law also includes principles of human rights, like the protection of life, property, and religious freedom.

As history progresses, so do the ideologies and mindsets of people. The Enlightenment period in Europe sought the emergence of new ideas about individual rights and freedoms. The French Revolution of 1789 and the American Revolution of 1776 were influenced by Enlightenment ideas and helped establish new legal frameworks for protecting individual rights. Due to the endless bloodshed for human rights, nations decided to come together to form a peaceful union known as the United Nations. Their goal is to create and maintain international peace and security (United Nations, n.d.). Therefore, in the 20th century, several key international treaties helped to establish the modern framework for human rights. The Universal Declaration of Human Rights, adopted by the United Nations in 1948, outlines a set of basic human rights that should be protected by all nations. Other important treaties include the International Covenant on Civil and Political Rights and the International Covenant on Economic, Social, and Cultural Rights. Despite the progress that has been made in protecting human rights, there are still many contemporary issues that pose challenges to the realization of human rights. These issues include systemic discrimination of marginalized communities, poverty, political repression, and environmental degradation. These are just a few examples of the many contemporary human rights issues that are being faced around the world. It requires continuous efforts from everyone to provide just human rights for all.

Ethics and human rights are two interrelated concepts that are central to understanding how we can live together in a just and equitable society. Ethics refers to the study of moral principles and values, while human rights are the basic rights and freedoms that all human beings are entitled to, regardless of nationality, ethnicity, religion, or gender. Throughout history, different cultures and civilizations have developed their ethical frameworks and understandings of human rights. From ancient Greece to the modern era, there have been significant advancements in our understanding and application of ethics and human rights. However, many contemporary issues still pose significant challenges to realising these ideals, such as discrimination, poverty, and political repression. Addressing these issues will require ongoing efforts from individuals, communities, and governments to promote human dignity, equality, and justice for the current and future generations to come.

References

Alexander, L., & Moore, M. (2020, October 30). Deontological ethics. Stanford Encyclopedia of Philosophy. Retrieved from https://plato.stanford.edu/entries/ethics-deontological/

Ayala, F. J. (2010). The difference of being human: Morality. Proceedings of the National Academy of Sciences, 107(supplement_2), 9015–9022. doi: 10.1073/pnas.0914616107

Baghramian, M., & Carter, J. A. (2020, September 15). Relativism. Stanford Encyclopedia of Philosophy. Retrieved from https://plato.stanford.edu/entries/relativism/

Britannica, T. Editors of Encyclopaedia (2013, June 16). nous. Encyclopedia Britannica. Retrieved from https://www.britannica.com/topic/philosophy-of-law/Conclusion

Bristow, W. (2017, August 29). Enlightenment. Stanford Encyclopedia of Philosophy. Retrieved from https://plato.stanford.edu/entries/enlightenment/

Cornell Law School. (n.d.). Ethics. Legal Information Institute. Retrieved from https://www.law.cornell.edu/wex/ethics

Den Uyl, D. J., Levy, J. T., & Surprenant, C. W. (2021). The essential: Enlightenment. Fraser Institute.

Diano, C. (n.d.). Epicureanism. Encyclopædia Britannica. Retrieved from https://www.britannica.com/topic/Epicureanism/The-Epicurean-school

Hursthouse, R., & Pettigrove, G. (2022, October 11). Virtue ethics. Stanford Encyclopedia of Philosophy. Retrieved from https://plato.stanford.edu/entries/ethics-virtue/

Hursthouse, R., & Pettigrove, G. (2022, October 11). Virtue ethics. Stanford Encyclopedia of Philosophy. Retrieved from https://plato.stanford.edu/entries/ethics-virtue/

Lewis, D. Malcolm (2023, February 10). Pericles. Encyclopaedia Britannica. Retrieved from https://www.britannica.com/biography/Pericles-Athenian-statesman

Merriam-Webster. (n.d.). Ethic. In the Merriam-Webster.com dictionary. Retrieved from https://www.merriam-webster.com/dictionary/ethic

Merriam-Webster. (n.d.). Human rights. In the Merriam-Webster.com dictionary. Retrieved from https://www.merriam-webster.com/dictionary/human%20rights

New International Version. (2011). Life Church. https://www.bible.com/bible/111/JHN.15.12-15.NIV Pigliucci, M. (n.d.). Stoicism. Internet encyclopaedia of philosophy. Retrieved from https://iep.utm.edu/stoicism/

Resnik, D. (2020). What is Ethics in Research & Why is it important? National Institute of Environmental Health Sciences. Retrieved from https://www.niehs.nih.gov/research/resources/bioethics/

whatis/index.cfm

Silk, M. (1984). Notes on the Judeo-Christian tradition in America. American Quarterly, 36(1), 65. doi: 10.2307/2712839

United Nations. (1948, November 14). 30 articles on the 30 articles of the Universal Declaration of Human Rights. OHCHR. Retrieved February 28, 2023, from https://www.ohchr.org/en/press-releases/2018/11/30-articles-30-articles-universal-declaration-human-rights

United Nations. (n.d.). Our work. United Nations. Retrieved March 1, 2023, from https://www.un.org/en/our-work

Chapter 2: Theories of Ethics

John Christy Johnson

Introduction

In the previous chapter, we have learned about the importance of ethics and particularly in consideration of our world's history and the concept of inalienable human rights that belong to all of us, as tenants of this globe. However, it is equally important to realise and understand some of the prevailing theories that have sought to explain and philosophically make sense of ethical principles. This chapter will revolve more so around the "how" or by extension, the condition or qualities of ethics that render its value.

Theories of ethics are essentially attempts to provide cohesive and cogent explanations of moral obligations that we have to ourselves and others. Here, we will discuss five of the more commonly accepted conventional theories of ethics; namely:

- Utilitarianism,
- deontology,
- virtue ethics,
- care ethics,
- and relativism.

Within these normative theories, there exist many sub-branches which will not be a focus as it is quite exhaustive and the object of this chapter is to instead provide a primer for the discussions of ethics and morals encountered in future chapters. Instead, I have provided definitions, etymologies, and examples, whether they be in the form of ethical dilemmas or analogies to supplement, each of the theories.

Utilitarianism

Utilitarianism, etymologically stems from the root word "utility," emphasising an ethic that places importance on the consequence or results of an action. It takes a computational approach to all the parties involved in a moral situation and summates their interests to develop a course of action that ensures the "greatest good for the greatest number." In the final analysis, utilitarianism weighs the benefits and harms of a decision and selects the one that maximises benefits while minimising harms.

To illustrate the appeal of utilitarianism, the "trolley problem" (described extensively by Thomson, 1985) has been popularly used. (Andrade 2019) The "trolley problem" is a moral dilemma that involves a situation in which people must make an emergency decision to save five lives at the cost of one. In this scenario, a runaway trolley with failed brakes is en route to kill five workers on the rail track. By pulling a lever, one can effectively divert the course of the trolley and direct it towards a track where there is only one worker. In doing so, the moral actor can save five lives in exchange for killing another. A study done in *Science* (Greene *et. al*, 2001) demonstrated that most people deem that it is appropriate to pull the lever. Although it is difficult to generalise these moral dilemmas to our larger socio-ecological environment, they provide a good glimpse into the inner workings of how we create value judgements of good and evil.

We can examine similar ethical dilemmas to highlight one of the flaws of utilitarianism, as well. One of the variants of the "trolley problem" involves being in a similar situation but in this case, rather than pulling a lever, the only way to stop the trolley is to push a fatter man in front of its course. In doing so, this man will die but this action can save the five others. Perhaps because there is an aversion for us to the physical act of pushing a person in the way of danger, more respondents are reluctant to select this option. (Tannsjo, 2015; Andrade 2019)

Oftentimes, the utilitarian position is portrayed as cold-hearted and calculative. However, there can be a utility (no pun intended) in this perspective when policymaking or determining what is the best decision at the population level. Positive historical events like the women's suffrage movement that have allowed people to function and benefit from equal rights and say in decision-making can be traced back to utilitarian ideologies that seek the greatest good for the greatest number. But at the same time, it is impossible to satisfy every person's needs and there are times when difficult choices must be made for the betterment of a greater number of people. Nevertheless, there are also other examples in history of fascist regimes like the Nazis and Soviet Russia where the utilitarian position has endangered the safety of others. Regardless of these events, utilitarianism remains a central tenet of several codified laws of governance and policy we see today, just like the next ethical theory we will discuss.

Deontology

Deontology is often attributed to the philosopher Immanuel Kant, who held that there were certain absolute, universal moral laws. The etymology of the word deontology is derived from the Greek words for duty (*deon*) and logic (*logos*).

In contrast to utilitarianism, the deontological perspective does not take into account the results produced by an action but instead focuses on the action itself. In this manner, most deontological theories tend to assert that some choices are inherently evil and cannot be justified, regardless of how morally good the consequences they may produce are.

Consider another ethical dilemma. Imagine a scenario where there is a perfectly healthy individual who presents to you, a capable surgeon. Five patients are waiting for life-saving organ transplants and these individuals' organs can be conveniently transplanted with a good prognosis for all five. To further complicate (or ease) the decision, this individual is a traveller and if you, as a surgeon, were to kill this man, no one would associate the murder with you. In effect, the only culpability you have would be the one imposed by self or deontology. Although a pure utilitarian may deem that the benefits would far outweigh the risks i.e. five lives saved vs one life lost, is there not a moral duty to self and neighbour that would be violated when you kill this otherwise innocent life?

Some more recent, interesting work by Hashimoto *et al* (2022) suggests that there may be some differences between utilitarian and deontological thinking that can be traced back to the system level. The Hashimoto group looked at the effect of time pressure in the setting of making some of these moral judgements. The two psychological processes they identified were intuitive and deliberative reasoning. Intuitive reasoning, or system 1 thinking, was often noted as quicker, generally rationalised more emotionally, and appealed to deontology. In direct contrast, deliberative reasoning, or system 2 thinking, was slower, cognitive, effortful, and appealed to utilitarianism. The authors suggest that the human mind operates as a dual processor in this regard when making decisions and time limitations play a role in making such choices. Another part of this study looked at peer pressure and the way these decisions changed after group deliberation. Interestingly, after group deliberation, the utilitarian decisions were shown to decrease.

Virtue Ethics

Virtue Ethics, unlike the previous two theories, emphasises neither the consequences (as in utilitarianism) nor the duty (as in deontology), but instead focuses on the virtue of the actor in question. Virtue ethics put the morality of the character deciding at the forefront. At its heart, this ethical theory rejects characterizations of virtue as a mere tool that may lead to good consequences or another trait coupled with moral duty and centralises virtues and vices as the animating spirit of ethics.

To cite an example, ethicists Mark White and Robert Arp has referred to the film *The Dark Knight* (White & Arp, 2018). The film follows the eponymous superhero Batman in his battle against the homicidal clown, the Joker. At one point in the storyline, Batman has an opportunity to kill the Joker, thereby plausibly saving the lives of many innocents. While the utilitarian sees the killing justified, and deontology would oppose killing anyone as morally reprehensible, the virtue ethicist would look at Batman, the agent in question. Batman does not want to sink to the Joker's level, so to speak. Killing Joker would not only go against the deontological notion that "killing is evil, but" it would also go against Batman's ethics as someone who would kill to maintain peace and order.

The main objections to virtue ethics have been around the lack of a universal code of rules and principles. In application, it would be difficult to codify and apply this ethical theory into formalised rules and laws to live by. For example, consider a virtuous human like Batman who assumes responsibility for the fictional town of Gotham City. Does the fact that he has the valour and performs heroic acts excuse him from acts of deception, violence, and opposition to authority? Perhaps, there is some creative licence and idolization of superheroes on our part as the audience to do so, but in the confines of the real world, it is difficult to rationalise some of the choices Batman makes. The virtue ethicist concerns themselves with virtue and vice and this can come at odds with the notions of good and evil.

Care Ethics

Care Ethics, in juxtaposition to virtue ethics, puts the notion of self as a moral character, within the context of interpersonal relationships. How do we as participants of relationships take responsibility for our dependencies and lack thereof? Care ethics posits that the actions we take part in the world are created by choices that involve providing or receiving care to a multi-layered network of individuals and communities. Care is often defined as a notion that involves maintaining the order of the world, and meeting the needs of oneself (i.e., self-care) and others.

Care ethics are thought to have been rooted in the feminist movement from the notion that there are certain duties that we have for one another. For example, there is a parental responsibility for fathers and mothers to take care of their children and vice versa, a sense of responsibility that offspring may have to support ageing parents. Care ethics, by definition, revolves around the fundamental idea that vulnerable parties require more attention when decisions are made.

During the feminist era, one of the prevailing theories was around the role of women and the idea that they were oppressed in civil society. In thinking about care, women were more vulnerable at the time and others in civil society had a responsibility to make accommodations for them. In a more pertinent local example, think about collective rights given to the Aboriginal peoples of Canada. The Aboriginals have faced injustices enacted on them by Canada's governmental programs such as the residential schools that assimilated, indoctrinated, and abused young Aboriginals in educational institutions. To rectify the errors, Canada's government has taken various efforts ranging from public apologies to subsidies to care for the vulnerable groups that have suffered and continue to suffer from the legacies of historical inequity and injustice. While these discussions of accommodations and collective rights remain contentious, the role of care ethics is perceptible in the context of treaty negotiations and the Truth and Reconciliation Council, established to create peace with the multicultural makeup of Canada.

An alternate variant of the trolley dilemma is to imagine if instead of the five workers and one worker, it was five strangers and the person on the other track was your mother or another loved one. Most people would have strong ties with family members and significant others and as biassed creatures, people's care ethics dictate that certain people in our life are more important than others. (Tannsjo, 2015; Andrade 2019)

Here is another similar, more familiar thought experiment. Imagine you are going camping with your daughter and a niece of a similar age. You have instructed both girls to steer clear of the lake waters as the currents can turn dangerous quickly. Unfortunately, both girls, being at a mischievous age, ignore your advice and get caught up in the raging waters. You know that your daughter is a better swimmer than your niece. Given that your daughter may be able to rescue herself, should you save your niece or daughter? In this situation, you have a responsibility as a caregiver to both girls but perhaps the connection forged with a daughter is more important than a niece, pushing you to reach your arm out to your daughter first.

The contemporary application of care ethics is most readily applicable in the setting of healthcare. Medical ethics, although they have largely evolved with the advent of medical techniques, surgery, and the use of pharmaceuticals. Today, the moral obligations of care are represented by four pillars that provide us with some valuable insight into the healthcare provider's (care provider's) duty towards the patient (vulnerable). Without going down the rabbit hole of medical-legal issues, the four ethical pillars of healthcare are:

1. Beneficence: which translates to "do good,"
2. non-maleficence which translates to "not harm"
3. autonomy or patient-involved care,
4. and justice which centres around providing fair care

Interestingly enough, it is apparent that these principles parallel or borrow from some of the other ethical theories such as utilitarianism (beneficence and non-maleficence) and deontology (justice), and virtue ethics (autonomy). That being said, the overarching theme of these principles goes back to supporting the patient-healthcare provider relationship. One of the other sides these principles do not adequately address is the responsibility of the patient to the healthcare provider. Providers also deserve to be treated with respect and today, there is an increasing awareness of provider burnout, abuse, and overwork. This is in line with another of the critiques of care ethics - it is difficult to operate on a clear dichotomy between caregiver and provider, especially concerning the physician-patient relationship.

Relativism

Relativism is based on a concept that differs from all previously discussed normative theories of ethics. Relativism creates a transmutable form of ethics that is context-dependent. The same choice or course of action in one situation may be morally reprehensible in society A but becomes morally acceptable in society B. From a relativistic perspective, proponents may appreciate the adaptational view that different contexts necessitate different ethics and ought to be changed for the sake of the situation. Opponents could argue that ethics should not be merely decided upon by the whims of culture but should be foundational, strict unalterable notions.

However, consider how even within a single country, there are different legislations and perspectives on what rights and responsibilities their citizens should have. For example, abortion legislation differs from state to state in the United States regarding who should have the right to abort and at what gestational age in the pregnancy.

When dealing with relativist arguments, semantics is at the heart of various formulations of relativism. Sometimes, relativism is classified as either content relativism or truth relativism. Content relativism is the semantic doctrine that asserts the content of an asserted statement is determined by the context in which it is made, whereas truth relativism is the doctrine that the truth of a particular statement is determined by the context in which it is made.

For example, there is an old parable called the "Blind men and the elephant" that refers to this concept, perhaps unknowingly. In this story, as the name suggests, there are multiple blind men and an elephant. Each blind man feels a different part of the elephant and describes it as a different item. This includes a pot (the elephant's head), a winnowing basket (ear), a ploughshare (tusk), a plough (trunk), a granary (body), a pillar (foot), a mortar (back), a pestle (tail) and a brush (tip of the tail). Relative to one blind man, the other blind men's descriptions of the elephant are false and their own is true. From a content relativism perspective, this would mean that the assertion that an elephant's head is a mere consequence of the context of a blind man perceiving the world from his other senses. From a truth relativism perspective, this would suggest that the assertion that an elephant's head is a pot is a subjective truth concerning the blind person, as this is their only means of making sense of the world.

The critiques of relativism, albeit many, tend to revolve around the nature of how morality should not be transmutable. There is a slippery slope that comes with being able to change the rules to suit one's needs and ulterior motives can poison the ethical essence. To address the elephant in the room (pun intended), returning to our parable, can we truly deny the reality of the situation that there is an elephant? At the same time, perhaps even our third-party view of seeing an elephant and blind men is but an illusion of our limitations in perceiving the world. After all, how do we know that we are not merely brains in a vat being fed stimuli and instead active agents that enact change to our environments?

Conclusion

Moral judgments are not easy and can be challenging to make, especially within the context and constraints of a highly sophisticated socio-ecological landscape with limited resources, time, and bandwidth. Our brains can be clouded by biases, virtues, vices, expectations, and other external pressures. Theories of ethics serve as handrails, by no means comprehensive or fool-proof, but remain a testament to the human condition and our ability to differentiate good and evil. Throughout this chapter, we discussed utilitarianism, deontology, virtue ethics, care ethics, and relativism. While these theories are some of the most popular ones, they are by no means the only ones or necessarily, the morally superior ones.

Humanism, the Renaissance, the feminist movement, and landmark medical legislations amongst other historical events have inspired many of these theories. It is important to understand some of the historical significance and context of these ethical thinkers, as described in the previous chapter, to fully understand and appreciate the value of such ethical philosophies. Furthermore, it is equally important to recognize that some of these theories may or may not hold for contemporary society. As we have modernised and digitised data, more online interactions than ever, and access to more readily digestible information, it becomes increasingly complex to navigate the intricacies of technology, politics, and the justice system. As you continue to read the next chapters, keep in mind these theories and see for yourself if they hold in these other contexts.

References

Andrade G. (2019). Medical ethics and the trolley problem. *J Med Ethics Hist Med, 12*(3). Retrieved from https://www.ncbi.nlm.nih.gov/pmc/articles/PMC6642460/

Greene, Joshua D., et al. "An fMRI investigation of emotional engagement in moral judgement." Science 293.5537 (2001): 2105-2108. doi: 10.1126/science.1062872

Hashimoto H, Maeda K, Matsumura K. Fickle Judgments in Moral Dilemmas: Time Pressure and Utilitarian Judgments in an Interdependent Culture. *J. Front Psychol.* 3(13):732-795. doi: 10.3389/fpsyg.2022.795732

Tannsjo T. Taking life: Three Theories on the Ethics of Killing. UK: Oxford University Press; 2015.

Thomson, Judith Jarvis. "The trolley problem." Yale LJ 94 (1984): 1395. doi: 10.2307/796133

White MD, Arp R. Should Batman Kill the Joker? The Boston Globe (2008) The Norton Sampler: Short Essays for Composition 8. Retrieved from http://archive.boston.com/bostonglobe/editorial_opinion/oped/articles/2008/07/25/should_batman_kill_the_joker/

Chapter 3: International Human Rights Instruments

Annilea Purser

Introduction

Those disengaged from international politics, or even just political life in general, may be unaware of what might occur in the case that their human rights are violated. As previous chapters have explained, human rights are complex, difficult to define, and dependent on one's positionality in society, such as their geographic location or identity. Yet, the bottom line – which is most simply defined by the United Nations – is that human rights "are inherent to all human beings," (United Nations, n.d.). Considering the aforementioned vast unawareness of human rights protections and the relatively reductionist definition of what human rights exactly are, it is imperative to question how these rights are protected daily.

Internationally, there exist hundreds of human rights instruments that work to build, uphold, and sometimes, reinforce human rights on a global scale. Here, much like the term "human rights" itself, "instruments" is a broad term, which in this chapter will be used to describe the declarations, treaties, and other forms of literature that are deployed as the means of a basis for human rights law on an international scale. As eloquently described by the Icelandic Human Rights Centre, the international form of human rights instruments emerged out of a series of interesting conditions which will be explored further throughout the subsections of this chapter. It should be noted, however, that much of the context of why international human rights instruments were created was due to the shared consensus that some sort of balance needed to be achieved between regional and domestic human rights instruments, particularly in European countries.

With such an ideal came the rise in the number of international human rights instruments, with some of the most remarkable stemming from the United Nations. International human rights mechanisms coming from the United Nations, or being initiated by UN countries, are unsurprising (United Nations, n.d). Simply put, the United Nations was developed as the predecessor of the League of Nations following the second world war, with the stated goal of maintaining international peace and security (United Nations, n.d). Further, said the goal is said to be achieved by working on numerous human rights-related efforts such as generally protecting human rights at large, supporting humanitarian aid with the United Nations Office for the Coordination of Humanitarian Affairs, or supporting the security of longer-term human rights protections efforts through programs like the Sustainable Development Goals (formerly, Millennium Development Goals) (United Nations, n.d).

Interestingly, the sheer size, capacity, and scope of the United Nations have resulted in the UN Human Rights Office of The High Commissioner developing and upholding a vast array of International Human Rights Instruments. Amongst the most prominent, UN-based Human Rights Instruments include: the Universal Declaration of Human Rights (UDHR) developed in 1948, the International Covenant on Civil and Political Rights (ICCPR) developed in 1976, the International Covenant on Economic, Social and Cultural Rights (ICESCR) entered into force in 1976, and the Convention against Torture and Other Cruel, Inhuman or Degrading Treatment or Punishment (CAT) which entered into force later, in 1987 (United Nations, n.d). Considering the influence of these four International human rights instruments and their prestige as they relate to the world's most influential international organization – the United Nations – it is important to assess their histories, purposes, memberships, influences, and certain important points of contention that have existed relating to them.

Universal Declaration of Human Rights (UDHR)

The Universal Declaration of Human Rights is the most significant human rights instrument to exist. The UDHR was formally enacted on December 10th of 1948 in the General Assembly, thus being the first order of business pursued by the UN (United Nations, n.d). The foundations behind why the UDHR was developed are important to understanding the development process and where the international institution stands today. Put simply, the foundation of the UDHR and the United Nations as a whole was to foster an international community that protects human rights (United Nations, n.d). This is furthered by the context in which this notion was put forth: right after the second world war (United Nations, n.d). During this time, countries witnessed the horrific actions taken during things like the Holocaust, and the significant loss of life and security, which prompted them to develop protections against future atrocities, the ideology being that if countries sign onto an agreement, communicate about conflicts, and "work together," then they are less likely to fight one another or engage in human rights violations (United Nations, n.d). Such realization of the abilities of countries to act wickedly or morally corrupt was echoed by scholars at the time, albeit sometimes reaching different conclusions on what actions should be taken to counter evil forces (United Nations, n.d).

Prominent writer Hannah Arendt (1906-1975) – who was born into a German-Jewish family – was a political philosopher who witnessed the brutality of the second world war, more particularly, the effects of the Holocaust (Passerin, 2006). Those unfamiliar with Arendt herself may be reminded of certain notable, well-known works that she published like The Origins of Totalitarianism, The Human Condition, The Life *of the Mind*, and *Eichmann in Jerusalem: A Report on the Banality of Evil* (Passerin, 2006). While Arendt is most aligned with the realist school of thought – alongside others writing at the time like Hans Morgenthau – that contrasts the liberal institutionalist nature of the United Nations and, more broadly, the idea of international human rights instruments as a whole, she is relevant to this discussion of the UDHR because she proposed the idea of the banality of evil (Passerin, 2006). In this, the banality of evil can simply be understood as the seemingly benign nature of "evil" and the fact that humans can commit major atrocities against other humans. Arendt's opinion, which as aforementioned, was written during the aftermath of the second world war, was shared by many nations of the world. In other terms, countries globally were faced with the question: now that we know we are capable of such atrocities, how do we ensure that they never occur again?" Again, this isn't to say that Arendt was aligned with the ideology that a global body of governance (in this case, the UN) nor that an international human rights institution (in this case, the UDHR) could be effective in dealing with this question, but countries of the world turned to liberal institutionalism did turn to this solution (United Nations, n.d).

This is where the idea of the UDHR came from: to answer the essential question of how to deal with and work towards avoiding state atrocities that harm so many (United Nations, n.d). In 1946, the drafting committee of the UDHR (the UDHR formerly referred to throughout the development process by other names, but for simplicity referred to just as the UDHR here), was developed after the Commission on Human Rights allowed for the pursuit of a preliminary draft of an international bill of human rights (United Nations, n.d.). The drafting committee was formed of eight countries that were chosen based on certain considerations, such as geographical location (United Nations, n.d). In this sense, the geographical "spreading out" of committee members allowed certain country representatives to act as "anchors" for the further involvement and pursuit of gaining interest from other neighbouring countries – especially those less inclined to participate in human rights development activities (United Nations, n.d). The Commission itself was made up of 18 different members from various perspectives, with the leadership of the commission consisting of Eleanor Roosevelt, the former first lady to Franklin D. Roosevelt from the United States, René Cassin from France, Charles Malik from Lebanon, Pen Chung Chang from China, John Humphrey from Canada (United Nations, n.d). Despite her thorough challenges in the political sphere because of her gender, Eleanor Roosevelt acted as the key motivational force of the UDHR and the Chair of the commission (United Nations, n.d). Amongst those involved in the drafting committee, it is important to note how significant it was in a post-World War atmosphere to have major forces join together – with members from France, Chile, the United Kingdom, and Canada – despite the mass atrocities that had just occurred (United Nations, n.d).

Eventually, the drafting efforts of the instrument snowballed, until the official draft declaration, the Geneva draft, gathered input from over 50 UN member states (United Nations, n.d). In December of 1948, two years after the initiation of the process, the UDHR was enacted in the General Assembly located in Paris at the time, through resolution 217 A (III) (United Nations, n.d). Notably, no member states of the UN chose to dissent, but eight UN members did decide to abstain, those mainly being members of the Soviet Bloc, as well as South Africa which was under the brutal South African Nationalist Party that enforced apartheid, and Saudi Arabia who disagreed with the UDHR's position on religion, stating that it contrasted Islam ideals (United Nations, n.d). The UDHR is undoubtedly a historic landmark instrument for advancing human rights globally. Moving on from the formation of the UDHR, the document itself is quite expansive, featuring thirty unique articles on human rights protection (United Nations, 1948). While this summary simplifies the expansiveness of the UDHR, there are four key principles that all thirty of the articles adhere to, those being: universality, interdependence and indivisibility, equality, and non-discrimination (United Nations, n.d).

International Covenant on Civil and Political Rights (ICCPR)

While the major international human rights documents among the instruments discussed in the chapter are the UDHR, the International Covenant on Civil and Political Rights (ICCPR) and the International Covenant on Economic, Social and Cultural Rights (ICESCR) are also critical documents (United Nations OHCHR, n.d). During the same General Assembly that brought forth the declaration, it was motioned that, at the request of the Commission on Human Rights, the development of an international human rights covenant be produced (United Nations OHCHR, n.d). Originally, said the treaty would be pursued through a single document output, however, contention arose over combining civil rights with economic, social, and cultural rights as certain states were comfortable with pursuing either or, but not both, within their borders (United Nations OHCHR, n.d). Thus, committees took up these matters separately: one treaty on civil and political rights, and another on economic, social, and cultural rights (Project on Canada's HR Commitments, 2015). Regarding the former half – civil and political rights – the United Nations developed the ICCPR under General Assembly resolution 2200A (XXI) (United Nations OHCHR, n.d). The document itself was completed on December 16th of 1966, but was unable to be ratified until a whole ten years later on March 23rd of 1976 as they required 35 member states to sign on, and were unable to secure said states until then (Project on Canada's HR Commitments, 2015). Today, the ICCPR has 173 members signed onto it, with 6 countries without ratification – including China, Cuba, and North Korea, who also tried to withdraw from the covenant altogether (Project on Canada's HR Commitments, 2015). Topics covered by the ICCPR include freedoms like the freedom to speech, expression, religion, and association, as well as related rights like the right to life, liberty, and freedom from enslavement. The ICCPR has an average of three sessions per year, typically hosted in Switzerland and the Geneva office. After the signing of the covenant in 1976, two optional protocols came forth (Project on Canada's HR Commitments, 2015). The first – which was enacted the same day as the original ratification – prescribes that the covenant's Human Rights Committee can process complaints from citizens who have their civil and/or political rights infringed upon (Project on Canada's HR Commitments, 2015). The second optional protocol didn't come until July 11th of 1991 and called for all signed-on parties to remove the death penalty (Project on Canada's HR Commitments, 2015). The second optional protocol would prove to be difficult for member countries like the United States who continue to utilize the death penalty as a means of criminal punishment (Project on Canada's HR Commitments, 2015).

International Covenandt on Economic, Social, and Cultural Rights (ICESCR)

Flowing from the same General Assembly as the ICCPR, the covenant on economic, social, and cultural rights sets out to achieve similar objectives as the ICCPR, just related to a different type or section of human rights (United Nations OHCHR, n.d). The ICESCR was adopted in the same year as the ICCPR, 1966 (December 16th), but, again like the ICCPR, only came into force ten years later, on January 3rd of 1976 (United Nations OHCHR, n.d). The ICESCR was ratified by the required 35 member states on this date. Along with the original document, there is a single optional protocol to the ICESCR, often referred to as OP-ICESCR, that was ratified on May 5th of 2013 (United Nations OHCHR, n.d). The OP-ICESCR enables the Human Rights Committee to be able to consider complaints about economic, social, and political rights violations – that must be significant and systemic – from both individuals and states (inter-state) (United Nations OHCHR, n.d).

Presently, 171 states have now signed onto the Covenant, but only 43 have agreed to the new optional protocol (United Nations OHCHR, n.d). Notably, only 11 countries total had not ratified either the ICCPR or the ICESCR, those being: Bangladesh,

Burma, the Cook Islands, Fiji, Kiribati, Laos, Malaysia, Pakistan, Papua New Guinea, Samoa, Singapore, Tonga, Tuvalu, Vanuatu (United Nations OHCHR, n.d). However, it should be noted that this list has shifted, with states like Pakistan now signing onto both covenants. As the name suggests, the ICESCR instrument covers rights related to economic, social, and cultural provisions (United Nations OHCHR, n.d). Freedoms include the freedom from discrimination, to choose work, to choose your child's schooling, to not be hungry, and to pursue research (United Nations OHCHR, n.d). Rights include those such as the right to practice culture, pursue education, be healthy, live adequately, strike, have social security, form work unions, have gender equality, work, and more (United Nations OHCHR, n.d).

Convention against Torture and Other Cruel, Inhuman or Degrading Treatment or Punishment (CAT)

The last international human rights instrument to be explored in this chapter is the Convention against Torture and Other Cruel, Inhuman, or Degrading Treatment or Punishment, which is referred to as CAT or Torture Convention (Danelius, 2008). In December 1975, it was motioned within the General Assembly for the Commission on Human Rights to begin studying torture and its impacts, as well as future forms of treaties to protect against it (Danelius, 2008). Through resolution 39/46, the General Assembly adopted the CAT, with it coming into force three years later on June 26th, 1987, being ratified by only 20 states to begin (Danelius, 2008). Throughout the process of developing the CAT, roadblocks slowed its progress, such as difficulties in defining the term "torture" as some members thought it was too broad, what jurisdiction the CAT would have which was eventually decided upon as being international instead of state-based, and concerns over implementation which concluded with an opt-out clause – amongst other things – to allow states to disagree with when the CAT is being used (Danelius, 2008). In addition, the CAT also has an optional protocol that was ratified on December

18th, 1992 which, if agreed to by states, would allow UN officials to visit their detention centres regularly to ensure that no torture or torture-like practices were being used against citizens (Danelius, 2008). The CAT essentially places obligations on states to not torture their citizens or other individuals in their countries, ensure that those being removed from their country are not going to be subject to torture because of their removal, and commit to investigating suspected torture (Danelius, 2008). Presently, 173 states have ratified the CAT, the same number as the ICCPR, and two states higher than the ICESCR (n.a, 2017). Nine states have not ratified the CAT, including India, Sudan, Brunei, Bahamas, Sao Tome and Principe, Angola, Comoros, Gambia, and Palau (n.a., 2017).

Conclusion

Together, the Universal Declaration of Human Rights, the International Covenant on Civil and Political Rights, and the International Covenant on Economic, Social, and Cultural Rights form the international bill of rights (United Nations, n.d). The Convention against Torture and Other Cruel, Inhuman or Degrading Treatment or Punishment came at a later date to the international bill of rights documents but is nonetheless another important international human rights instrument flowing from the United Nations. While, undoubtedly, these documents were ground-breaking, they have not gone without their controversies and slew of points of contention since their inception in 1945 (Hoover, 2013). While the UN came at the close of the second world war, another war – one which would be more destructive and politically "hot" – was just around the corner: the Cold War. The importance of the Cold War was that it highlighted the U.S. hegemony and fear of the non-West that had largely been overlooked amongst the United Nations states that formed the declaration (Hoover, 2013). Said hegemony, which, of course, the Soviet Bloc countries were quick to critique even before the final UDHR signing, brought attention to questions of who the idea of "universal human rights" were for, resulting in questions like whose idea is the concept of human rights? Whom do human rights serve? Are human rights prescribed under the declaration truly universal? Those sceptical of the idea of universal human rights bring forth such questions.

One sceptic is Hoover (2013) who presents that the notion of universal human rights requires the allotment of authority as the definition of "universal" and "human rights" must flow from somewhere, and said context is critical in the later placing of authority (p. 223). Further, Hoover also brings forth the fact that the U.S. has been the central guiding state to developing the declaration – like with the aforementioned Eleanor Roosevelt being at the forefront of UDHR affairs – which has underscored the western-centricity of the documents (2013). Another major, related, point of contention is how the UDHR is applied. Continuing on the same line of critique, it has been highlighted throughout history how certain states – like Canada with Indigenous Peoples – have been offered leniency in how they apply human rights, whereas others, particularly non-Western countries, face much scrutiny and accusations of human rights offences under the declaration (Hoover, 2013). Such contestations remain highly political and debatable, even 77 years after the UDHR's initial signing, and are thus a worthwhile consideration to anyone studying human rights or international institutions. However, regardless of these controversies, international human rights institutions are a worthwhile study considering their vastness and implications on the international community as a whole.

References

Danelius, H. (2008, June). *Convention against Torture and Other Cruel, Inhuman or Degrading Treatment or Punishment - Main Page*. United Nations - Office of Legal Affairs. Retrieved from https://legal.un.org/avl/ha/catcidtp/catcidtp.html

India Among 9 Nations That Haven't Ratified UN Convention Against Torture. (2017, May 4). Outlook India. Retrieved from https://www.outlookindia.com/website/story/india-among-9-nations-that-havent-ratified-un-convention-against-torture/298749

Passerin, M. (2006, July 27). *Hannah Arendt (Stanford Encyclopedia of Philosophy)*. Stanford Encyclopedia of Philosophy. Retrieved from https://plato.stanford.edu/entries/arendt/

Project on Canada's Human Rights Commitments. (2015, November 10). *History of the International Covenant on Civil and Political Rights*. Canada's Human Rights Commitments. Retrieved from http://humanrightscommitments.ca/2015/11/history-of-the-international-covenant-on-civil-and-political-rights/

United Nations OHCHR. (n.d.). *Background to the Covenant*. OHCHR. Retrieved from https://www.ohchr.org/en/treaty-bodies/cescr/background-covenant

United Nations OHCHR. (n.d.). *Background to the International Covenant on Civil and Political Rights and Optional Protocols*. OHCHR. Retrieved from https://www.ohchr.org/en/treaty-bodies/ccpr/background-international-covenant-civil-and-political-rights-and-optional-protocols

United Nations. (n.d.). *History of the Declaration | United Nations*. the United Nations. Retrieved from https://www.un.org/en/about-us/udhr/history-of-the-declaration

United Nations. (n.d.). *Human Rights | United Nations*. the United Nations. Retrieved from https://www.un.org/en/global-issues/human-rights

United Nations. (n.d.). *The Foundation of International Human Rights Law | United Nations*. the United Nations. Retrieved from https://www.un.org/en/about-us/udhr/foundation-of-international-human-rights-law

Chapter 4: National Human Rights Institutions

Jason Zhou

Introduction

National Human Rights Institutions or NHRIs are independent organisations funded by governments to promote and protect human rights within their own countries. The goal of NHRIs is to ensure that human rights are respected, protected, and fulfilled for everyone within their jurisdiction regardless of their race, ethnicity, gender, religion, or any other status. NHRIs provide advice and recommendations to the government based on the United Nations reports and resolutions. They implement international human rights standards at the national level and can take on various forms such as commissions, ombudsmen, human rights centres, or institutes. The mandate of each NHRI can vary from country to country but work to promote and protect human rights. NHRIs are designed to monitor, investigate, and report on human rights abuses within their jurisdiction. National Human Rights Institutions must adhere to the global standards set out in the Paris Principles adopted in 1993 by the United Nations General Assembly.

Mandate and Responsibilities

The mandate of each National Human Right Institution differs based on the country in which they are established. The general mandate of NHRIs is to protect and promote the rights of everyone within their country. The mandates focus on groups who face a greater risk of human rights violations (NHRIs 2022). The groups identified as at-risk are children, people with disabilities, human rights defenders, indigenous people, migrants, elderly, ethnic, religious, linguistic, and cultural minorities, refugees, and asylum seekers (Prioritising groups at risk of human rights violations). The main responsibilities of NHRIs are to report and investigate human rights violations, provide legal aid and assistance to victims of human rights abuses, promote public awareness of human rights, educate the public on human rights, advise the government of human rights policy and legislation, and make recommendations to the government for the protection and promotion of human rights. NHRIs are important to their countries because they hold an important role in ensuring governments are accountable for their human rights obligations and provide a mechanism for individuals or groups to address the government.

Education is a key part of a National Human Right Institution's responsibilities. The Global Alliance of National Human Rights Institutions or GANHRI states that "to exercise their rights and respect the rights of others, people first need to know their rights" meaning it is of utmost importance to ensure people know what rights they have (Responsibilities of NHRIs: Human rights education 2022). Human rights education aims to prevent future human rights violations by ensuring humans know when their rights are violated and how their rights are violated. Awareness of fundamental rights and freedoms helps people understand their rights and the rights of others empowering them to take action when their rights are violated. Education on human rights can also increase accountability and tolerance. One of the international standards set out by the United Nations Human Rights Office of the High Commissioner or OHCHR is the freedom of religion or belief (International standards). By educating the population on individual rights, the diversity of human experience, and the importance of respecting differences, the individual is less likely to engage in discriminatory behaviour and become more tolerant. Accountability is increased because individuals will know to hold others and themselves accountable for noticing when human rights abuses occur. Education is a fundamental part of the mandate of NHRIs as education in human rights helps create a culture of social justice that assists in speaking out against injustice, challenges discriminatory practices, and advocates for positive human rights changes leading to a more equitable world.

Another key responsibility of National Human Rights Institutions is to guide the government by providing advice and recommendations. OHCHR's Principles Relating to the Status of National Institutions states that "a national institution shall be vested with competence to promote and protect human rights" (1993) and that a national institution should have the following responsibility "to promote and ensure the harmonization of national legislation, regulations and practices with the international human rights instruments to which the State is a party, and their effective implementation" (1993). Meaning, it is the NHRI's responsibility to ensure that any resolution by the United Nations that advances human rights will be advocated by the NHRI to ensure that they are implemented nationally and that the government follows through with international human rights standards. The UN provides a framework for action, guidance, and direction on human rights issues and NHRIs advocate for the alignment of policy and legislative changes to international human rights standards.

In addition, NHRIs can assist governments in resolving conflicts and disputes that arise as a result of human rights abuses. GANHRI states this responsibility as complaint handling. An NHRI's complaint-handling function needs to be accessible to all people. The complaint handling function varies based on the NHRI's founding legislation but generally includes, who can bring a complaint, who can respond to a complaint, how the complaint is resolved, and other matters such as time restrictions or restrictions related to court proceedings (Responsibilities and functions of NHRIs: Complaint handling 2022). To ensure the

NHRI can handle investigations, they should be granted adequate powers such as taking and handling evidence from victims and witnesses, compelling the attendance of a witness for the question, obtaining documents and information and being able to enter premises to conduct inspections (Responsibilities and functions of NHRIs: Complaint handling 2022). These powers of investigation ensure the NHRI can address legitimate complaints about human rights abuses. Furthermore, one of the key aspects of the Paris Principles is that NHRIs with complaint-handling functions should "seek... an amicable settlement through conciliation" (Responsibilities and functions of NHRIs: Complaint handling 2022). Meaning, NHRIs cannot make a binding decision but must seek conciliation

Monitoring and reporting human rights situations is another key responsibility of NHRIs. Tracking human rights abuses that have taken place allows NHRIs to provide better guidance and promote reform of laws, policies, and practices to prevent future human rights abuses from occurring. Furthermore, by gathering evidence of human rights abuses within a country, public awareness increases of human rights abuses and creates positive pressure for change. There is no specific method for an NHRI to monitor human rights situations, it depends on the country, the cultural background, and any microcultures. However, the responsibilities developed for monitoring human rights situations typically include monitoring elections and places of detention such as jails, labour camps, or prisons (Manual on National Human Rights Institutions 2018). If a human rights violation is found, the NHRI has a responsibility to increase visibility on the issue by gathering evidence, raising awareness, and advocating for change.

Paris Principles

The Paris Principles refer to a set of international standards adopted in 1993 by the United Nations General Assembly. The standards set out by the Paris Principles are the minimum that NHRIs must meet to be considered credible by the UN. The key pillars of the Paris Principles are pluralism, independence, and effectiveness. Pluralism is a key factor in the composition of an NHRI as pluralism ensures that the NHRI recognizes and accommodates the diversity of different viewpoints, beliefs, and lifestyles within a society. Independence from the government is important because it ensures the autonomy of the institution. NHRIs should be independent of the government and free from political interference, to carry out their mandate impartially, objectively, and effectively. Furthermore, NHRIs should have a clear and broad mandate to promote and protect human rights, and broad functions to be able to deliver on their mandates (Principles relating to the status of National Institutions (the Paris Principles) 1993). The standards set out by the Paris Principles ensure NHRIs are effective mechanisms for promoting and protecting human rights.

Structure of National Human Rights Institutions

The structure of a National Human Right Institution varies based on the country in which they are formed but can be commonly found as commissions, ombudsmen, human rights centres, or institutes. Additionally, the internal structures can vary as well, with some institutions focusing on a specific thematic responsibility such as racial equality, indigenous rights, women's rights, or children's rights. Despite all the differences in NHRIs, they all follow the minimum standards set out by the Paris Principles.

The most common type of NHRI is a commission. The commission-style model of NHRIs is commonly found in the Commonwealth countries, including Canada, Australia, and the United Kingdom or the United States of America. Commission-style models share common traits such as investigation of human rights abuses, having full-time paid staff, having broad mandates, receiving individual human rights abuse complaints also known as 'quasi-jurisdictional competence' in the Paris Principles and the authority to make recommendations to the government about human rights issues within the country. Human rights commissions often have several members with a chief commissioner at the top of the chain of command. Although there is a chief commissioner, decisions are made with several members ensuring diversity of membership and thoughts. Commission-style models are funded by the State and are given their mandate by law. Human rights commissions typically focus on quality rights and anti-discrimination work such as workplace equity (National Human Rights Institutions: History, Principles, Roles, and Responsibilities 2010).

The second most common type of NHRI is an ombudsman. This ombudsman model is commonly found in Eastern Europe, and Central and South America. Ombudsman models focus on conciliation to investigate and resolve human rights abuses. This model has been around before the idea of NHRIs. Ombudsman models follow the traditional 'Office of the Ombudsman model in which a single person is at the head and makes decisions. The benefit of this model is that resolutions are fast, however, investigations are not as formal. Due to having one person at the helm, this model is dependent on the public trust in the ombudsman him or herself. The reputation, integrity, leadership, and authority of the ombudsman are important factors in this model. Ombudsman models found in comparatively larger countries often have deputies who can make decisions as well. However, this model continues to share attributes with the commission-style model. Factors that are shared include state funding, investigation of human rights abuses, and making recommendations to the local government. The negatives to an ombudsman-style model are that it lacks the requirement for diversity, and a single leader does not meet plurality as per General Assembly resolution 63/169 on the role of the Ombudsman. Furthermore, if the Ombudsman is from a dominant group, minoritarians may not feel comfortable addressing their human rights issues. The methods to solve this problem include developing an advisory board or council for the ombudsman. The board or council could be made up of diverse members to increase the plurality of the ombudsman (National Human Rights Institutions: History, Principles, Roles, and Responsibilities 2010).

Hybrid models are NHRIs that have more than one mandate. Unlike the previously discussed models of commissions and ombudsman, hybrid models do not only focus on human rights but also address corruption, environmental issues, and maladministration. This model is commonly found in Latin American countries and Spain (National Human Rights Institutions: History, Principles, Roles, and Responsibilities 2010). Hybrid models are known to be an institution that combines human rights and traditional ombudsman functions. However, hybrid models share similar problems to ombudsman-style NHRIs in that they are headed by a single person. The advantage to a hybrid model is that because their mandate does not only focus on human rights, they can provide a 'one-stop' service across many issues. This can result in economies of scale and avoidance of additional infrastructure costs. For example, if a hybrid model includes a mandate of both protecting the environment and human rights, issues that affect both could be dealt with at the same location. The disadvantage of having such a wide mandate is that it could diminish the importance of human rights as human rights are fundamental and inalienable (National Human Rights Institutions: History, Principles, Roles, and Responsibilities 2010).

Cooperation With International Bodies

The Global Alliance of National Human Rights Institution or GANHRI was created on December 13th, 1993 to promote and protect human rights. It is a network of independent NHRIs that are recognized by the United Nations as being authorized to protect and promote human rights within their respective jurisdictions. Since 2022, GANHRI brings over 115 NHRIs from across the globe to provide leadership and support in the promotion and protection of human rights (History of GANHRI and NHRIs 2023). GANHRI hosts an Annual Meeting to discuss problems facing human rights, human rights defenders, and best practices in the field of human rights, and provide support to fellow institutions.

GANHRI also provides accreditation to NRHIs based on their compliance with the Paris Principles. The accreditation process is a part of GANHRI's mandate and is delivered by the Sub-Committee on Accreditation or SCA. The goal of accreditation is to ensure NHRIs' are following the guidelines set out by the Paris Principles (A Practical Guide To the Work of The Sub-Committee On Accreditation (SCA) 2018). The accreditation process assesses how the Paris Principles are applied in law and practice. Questions such as, whether is the NHRI mandated by law, if the organisational structure of the NHRI is effective, and whether the NHRI can carry out its mandate effectively, independently, and without interference are asked. The SCA also understands that the quality of the service delivered by the NHRI can be affected by the context in which the NHRI is operating, factors such as the political state of the country, the economy, and state infrastructure are considered when accrediting. Therefore, the SCA treats each NHRI accreditation independently and can recognize in exceptional cases that NHRI may not be able to fully comply with the Paris Principles due to the volatile political situation in the NHRIs jurisdiction. If an NHRI is unable to meet the standards set out in the Paris Principles, the SCA will emphasise that the NHRI must have a plan or have taken steps to ensure individuals still have access to address human rights violations (A Practical Guide To the Work of The Sub-Committee On Accreditation (SCA) 2018).

The SCA is composed of four members, with one member coming from each of the GANHRI regions, Africa, North and South America, Asia Pacific, and Europe. Members of the SCA must be accredited at the highest level by the SCA. These members of the SCA are elected every three years and have no term limits. The SCA also has permanent observers including the OHCHR functioning as the Secretariat, a representative from each regional network, and a staff member from the GANHRI Head Office. The application process to be accredited starts with the NHRI contacting the SCA. The NHRI will have to provide an application portfolio outlining the legislation, organisational structure, annual budget, and a copy of the NHRI's most recent annual report.

The Secretariat will then review the application and if approved, the SCA will review the NHRI based on its criteria. Afterwards, the SCA provides recommendations to the NHRIs to follow to meet the standards set out. The accreditation is ranked in levels, with A being fully compliant with the Paris Principles, B being semi-compliant with the Paris Principles, and C not meeting the Paris Principles. There is additionally another status for no applications for accreditation (A Practical Guide To the Work of The Sub-Committee On Accreditation (SCA) 2018). Accreditation by the SCA is a rigorous process that ensures NHRI meets the standards set out by the Paris Principles and that NHRIs can protect and promote human rights for all individuals within their jurisdiction.

National Human Rights Institutions at Work

NHRIs protect and promote human rights within their jurisdiction, within Canada, the Canadian Human Rights Commission or CHRC has the mandate to promote human rights through research and policy, and protect human rights through a fair and effective complaint process (About Us - Canadian Human Rights Commission 2023). One of the primary goals of the CHRC is to promote pay equity. In 2020, a woman in Canada earned 89 cents for every dollar a man earned, or is equivalent to an 11% wage gap (What is Pay Equity 2021). As such, the Government of Canada created a Pay Equity commissioner who resolves issues relating to discrepancies in pay. The Pay Equity Commissioner is a part of the CHRC. The Pay Equity unit then recommended to the Government of Canada to create a Pay Equity Act, this legislation ensures if two different jobs contribute equally to their employer's operations, both employees should be paid the same (What is Pay Equity 2021). The CHRC promoted human rights by ensuring equitable pay within Canada.

Another CHRC objective is the promotion of anti-racism. One of the key tenants of ensuring the CHRC can deliver on its mandate is to ensure the CHRC itself has an open, healthy, safe, and inclusive workspace that has the core principles of anti-racism. To achieve this goal, the CHRC has implemented an action plan outlining the tasks required to achieve anti-racism within the Commission. The plan includes establishing an internal committee of visible minorities, tying the action plan to performance management, and reporting regularly to the Commission staff on the plan's process (Anti-Racism Action Plan 2021). By implementing anti-racism policies within the CHRC, they increase internal accountability. Furthermore, the anti-racism work applies also to all Canadians, the plan outlines actively participating in the Government of Canada's anti-racism working groups and establishing a national network of stakeholders representing visible minorities to consult and provide updates on the work for the CHRC (Anti-Racism Action Plan 2021).

Conclusion

National Human Rights Institutions can vary based on the country in which they are established. However, the responsibility stays the same despite the location of the NHRI, they must focus on protecting and promoting the rights of everyone within their country, with a focus on at-risk groups. NHRIs are responsible for reporting and investigating human rights violations, providing legal aid and assistance to victims of human rights abuses, promoting public awareness and education on human rights, advising the government on human rights policy and legislation, and making recommendations to the government for the protection and promotion of human rights. The Paris Principles outline the standards NHRIs must follow and the SCA provides accreditation to those who meet the standards. NHRIs may vary in the structure, composition, and mandate the government has given them but, they must stay focused on ensuring governments are

accountable for human rights obligations and providing a mechanism for individuals or groups to address their
human rights complaints.

References

About Us - Canadian Human Rights Commission. Canadian Human Rights Commission. (2023, February 2). Retrieved from https://www.chrc-ccdp.gc.ca/en/about-us

Anti-Racism Action Plan. Canadian Human Rights Commission. (2021, September). Retrieved from https://www.chrc-ccdp.gc.ca/en/resources/publications/anti-racism-action-plan

Canadian Human Rights Commission. (2018). A Practical Guide To the Work of The Sub-Committee On Accreditation (SCA). GANHRI. Retrieved from https://ganhri.org/wp-content/uploads/2019/11/GANHRI-Manual_online1.pdf

History of GANHRI and NHRIs. GANHRI. (2023, February 27). Retrieved from https://ganhri.org/history-of-ganhri-and-nhris/

International standards. OHCHR. (n.d.). Retrieved from https://www.ohchr.org/en/special-procedures/sr-religion-or-belief/international-standards

Manual on National Human Rights Institutions. Asia Pacific Forum of National Human Rights Institutions. (2018). Retrieved from https://apf-prod.s3.amazonaws.com/media/resource_file/Manual_on_NHRIs_Oct_2018.pdf?AWSAccessKeyId=AKIA57J-6V557ISASX34R&Signature=TJJ87fz2BJeoyG38VmoqCkNdrXA%3D&Expires=1676516065

NHRIs. Global Alliance of National Human Rights Institutions | GANHRI. (2022, February 22). Retrieved from https://ganhri.org/nhri/

Principles relating to the status of National Institutions (the Paris principles). OHCHR. (1993). Retrieved from https://www.ohchr.org/en/instruments-mechanisms/instruments/principles-relating-status-national-institutions-paris

Prioritising groups at risk of human rights violations. Asia Pacific Forum. (n.d.). Retrieved from https://www.asiapacificforum.net/members/what-are-nhris/fact-sheet-11-vulnerable-groups/#:~:text=Some%20groups%20are%20identified%20internationally,religious%2C%20linguistic%20and%20cultural%20minorities

Responsibilities and functions of NHRIs: Complaint handling. GANHRI. (2022, January 17). Retrieved from https://ganhri.org/complaint-handling-nhris/

Responsibilities of NHRIs: Human rights education. Global Alliance of National Human Rights Institutions | GANHRI. (2022, January 17). Retrieved from https://ganhri.org/human-rights-education/

United Nations. (2010). *National Human Rights Institutions: History, principles, roles, and Responsibilities* (Ser. Professional Training Series No. 4).

What is Pay Equity? Canadian Human Rights Commission. (2021, August 31). Retrieved from https://www.payequitychrc.ca/en/about-act/what-pay-equity

Chapter 5: Human Rights and Public Administration

John Zizler

Introduction

Human rights and public administration, these two concepts have been interconnected in many ways throughout history. From a logical perspective, if human rights are to be implemented in society, it must be done through public administration. This requires collective support and good governance in implementing human rights. It is important to understand the cycle of creating human rights, implementing them into society, and most importantly protecting and upholding human rights. This is all done through public administration, which can be defined as the implementation of government policies. Government policies that, in a perfect democracy, stem from public opinion and the requests of the people. Throughout this chapter, topics revolving around human rights in the public sector, human rights and public policies, and general human rights issues will be discussed. The importance of good governance and human rights and the role of civil servants in protecting human rights will also be discussed. The goal is to spread awareness of human rights issues in public administration and to educate individuals on the issue. The secondary goal is to highlight the importance of good governance in human rights reforms, as well as in tackling corruption within and between the government. This will allow us to spread awareness of these issues.

Human Rights in the Public Sector

Human rights issues have always been at the forefront of many controversial issues in the public sector. Whether it be human rights violations in law enforcement, public transit, education, healthcare, or in the government. A common controversial issue is workplace human rights violations, and/or, child labour human rights violations internationally. Other human rights issues are seen in public education, healthcare, and in the workplace. With that being said, from an ethical and moral perspective, human rights are implemented to prevent the unfair treatment of any individual. Therefore, implementing human rights in the public sector is essential for the progression and protection of human rights. The public sector can be defined as the portion of the economy composed of all levels of government and government-controlled enterprises. (Wegrich, K, n.d.). This includes all government-owned businesses, agencies, and enterprises. Furthermore, public ownership is prominent in public transport, education systems, and healthcare services, which as we know, are funded by taxpayers. Since the public sector has such a great presence in society, it makes sense that human rights are important issues that must be addressed. Society needs the collective support of individuals to create change. These individuals need to be the eyes, ears, and voices of the public in an effort toward the common good of all people. These individuals are there to tackle injustice and uphold human rights. Some of the most important human rights in the public sector include the right to education, the right to healthcare, and the right to work. These rights are given without any limitations based on race, sex, religious beliefs, age, or any other demographic factors.

Human Rights Issues in Healthcare

Starting with issues in the healthcare systems. Human rights issues regarding healthcare have been in conversations for a good part of history and are still being discussed today. As we have seen in today's world, human rights issues can vary depending on the location, economy, particular situation, etc. From human rights violations in the public healthcare systems to marginalized populations who have no access to the proper healthcare whatsoever. Discrimination in the delivery of healthcare has also been prominent in many countries around the world. This leads to poor quality care, which can cause serious health consequences. Overt or implicit discrimination in the delivery of health services – both within the health workforce and between health workers and service users – acts as a powerful barrier to health services, and contributes to poor quality care (WHO, 2022). Most of these health conditions are seen in low-income poverty-level communities, whether it be in a developed or developing country. A lot of the time healthcare providers lack the resources to perform certain health procedures, which can end up being detrimental to the patient, often resulting in further health complications or even death. As mentioned previously, many of these issues arise in less fortunate countries, in troubled economies and public systems. Most of the time, human rights to healthcare are violated due to the lack of funding, lack of resources, and limited to no health insurance. Therefore, it is safe to conclude that financial reasons are the most common explanation for human rights violations regarding proper health care.

Human Rights Issues in Public Education

Moving on to human rights issues in public education. The public education sector has seen many human rights violations throughout history, particularly in less fortunate communities and countries around the world. Whether it be inadequate access to education, hazardous conditions in the school, or violence at school. Many of these marginalized communities don't have the proper education conditions available to them. This ultimately violates a human's right to learn, to educate, and to start/continue a career. The most impacted demographic would be the children of sub-Saharan Africa. They currently face many obstacles to their right to education. Not only has the state of the economy impacted the education system, but attacks on and violence in public education have also created a huge barrier to education. Children in at least 18 African countries are affected by attacks against education and the military use of their schools (*Africa: Prioritize Education to Safeguard Children's Rights*, 2021). The attacks on the education systems in these African countries are one of many unfortunate occurrences that disrupt the accessibility of education to these children. Another current issue is the impact of the pandemic on the economy, which has left millions of children forced to work in hazardous conditions to afford to go to school. The response to the pandemic has essentially caused a domino effect, which has opened the door to many obstacles, preventing millions of children from access to proper education. The use of online learning has had a long-lasting detrimental impact on children's and families' finances, with online learning being more expensive than the alternative. This certainly hasn't helped the already corrupt education system; it has just created more problems.

The most impacted sub-demographics are girls, children with disabilities, low-income families, and as mentioned before, those living in armed conflict areas. Many of these children are forced into child labour to pay for their education, especially during the pandemic. Consequently, the unfortunate reality of online learning has also increased the costs of education, which further bared many children from attending school. Furthermore, more specific human rights issues include girls and children with disabilities. Girls face discriminatory barriers to their education due to issues regarding pregnancy, parenthood, of child marriage. Whereas persons with disabilities don't have acceptable accommodation and with the current economic climate, are unfortunately one of the last priorities. These issues have more substance to them, which branch out into many other issues that sadly we won't cover. It is safe to conclude that some of the main reasons for the lack of education are financial and economic reasons, geopolitical reasons, and the overall state of the country.

Human Rights Issues in the Workplace

Lastly, human rights issues in the workplace. Human rights issues in the workplace can vary. Whether it be child labour, unethical working conditions, or unreasonable working hours. Human rights issues in the workplace can also vary depending on geographical location. One of the most notable global human rights issues includes the presence of child labour. Roughly 160 million children were subjected to child labour at the beginning of 2020, with 9 million additional children at risk due to the impact of COVID-19. This accounts for nearly 1 in 10 children worldwide (*Child Labour,* 2021). As you can see child labour is still very prominent, especially in many less fortunate countries, and there may be several reasons for this. Some companies would capitalize on cheap labour to lower costs, at the expense of these children. Another reason for child labour might be poverty conditions where children are forced to work to cover the living expenses for their families. Some may also be forced into hazardous work through human trafficking. Others may be forced to work to pay for their education, as mentioned previously. These are some of the many reasons children are forced to work at a young age. Although some of the time it may seem necessary for survival, there are many consequences of child labour. The most notable consequences include bodily harm, mental harm, and in some cases death. This ultimately compromises their fundamental rights and reduces their overall potential and limits their futures. It also strips them from their childhoods, which again, poses further complications in the upbringing of the child. Most will never recover from past trauma and their entire lives will be negatively impacted. This is why child labour is considered an important human rights issue that needs to be addressed and publicized.

An additional unethical issue would be dangerous working conditions. Saving on production costs at the expense of an individual's health. Many companies are given the incentive of decreasing costs. However, is it ethical for companies to compromise the health of their employees to reduce these costs? That's where basic human rights come into play. Countless instances of reported unsafe working conditions are seen in the fashion industry. Many fashion brands place their factories in these countries to lower their manufacturing costs, in return for a higher profit margin back home. They take advantage of the cheap labour and essentially exploit these workers for their benefit. Low wages, forced overtime, and health and safety conditions are some of the many issues. Employees usually work with no ventilation, breathing in toxic substances, inhaling fibre dust, or blasting sand in unsafe buildings (*Inhumane working conditions,* n.d.). Furthermore, employees also regularly receive verbal and physical abuse from their employers. These employers impose limited breaks, limited room for error, and forced overtime. In some cases, when they fail to meet their (unreachable) daily target they are insulted, denied breaks, or not allowed to drink water (*Inhumane working conditions,* n.d.). Many of these employees work countless hours only to barely have enough money to provide for their families. Even with overtime, employees are seen to be struggling financially. They are essentially stripping these individuals from basic human rights in return for profit. These unethical issues may also arise between companies and their customers. Making lower-quality products, cutting the cost of goods, to increase profit margins. Many of these issues can arise in manufacturing companies, for example, car manufacturing companies. An example would include reducing the quality of seatbelts to cut production costs. Compromising safety for a higher profit is the same issue that arises. That's where human rights and ethics come into play. Some companies are willing to sacrifice the quality of a product to reduce product costs. Ethics come into play when they're jeopardizing human life in exchange for a higher profit margin. This can lead us to the conclusion that most of these workplace human rights violations are profit driven. These employees are being exploited to benefit the respective company, a leader in a position of power, or the entire economy as a whole. With that being said, financial and economic reasons are the incentive behind this unfortunate reality seen across many parts of the world.

Role of Civil Servants in Protecting Human Rights

Now that we've discussed human rights issues in popular public sectors, we'll shift our attention to how civil servants can protect these human rights. The purpose of civil and public servants is to instil change and make difference in sectors of society that were discriminatory in the past. Their mission is to create and provide programs and services to create a positive change in society and public administration. They're also there to provide a channel of communication from the top to the bottom of society. With that being said, a major issue civil and public servants face is the protection of human rights. Their job is to actively seek and cover potential human rights violations to gain public support and garner attention for the issue. In general, anyone who takes time out of their day to promote and protect human rights can be viewed as a civil servant. Defending human rights is part of the job of civil servants, especially if they see an act of prejudice going on around them. Whether it be standing up for a co-worker who is being discriminated against or leading the human rights movement to stop child labour, human rights violations can range depending on the circumstance. In many cases, civil servants are viewed as human rights defenders since they're advocating for an entire population of people. Human rights defenders are the eyes, ears, and voices of their communities (*Who are human rights defenders*, n.d.). By doing so, civil servants can start a public movement on an important lingering issue if they gain the support of the public.

The main goal is trying to ensure it is a free, fair, and informed public debate about the policies that affect us (Who are human rights defenders, n.d.). However, an issue that can arise from free public debate is public censorship which is used to silence the public on a controversial issue. Censorship can come from a government, private institution, or other controlling bodies where silencing the public on an issue is in their best interest. This is the result of conflicting interests between the public and individuals in high positions of power and influence. Unfortunately, in some countries, the government or powerful corporate interests harass or try to discredit people who defend human rights and lock them out of public discussions and silence their voices (*Who are human rights defenders,* n.d.). Depending on the location and the country of origin a human rights movement arises from, there can be some cases where civil servants get attacked and imprisoned for starting public movements. This is another tactic a controlling body may use to silence the public crowd, by essentially eliminating the facilitator and/or the orchestrator of a significant public movement. As a reminder, an individual of high influence can be a problem for a government if there are conflicting interests between the two parties. Both are essentially there to influence the public in one way or another. Power is highly sought after.

Good Governance and Human Rights

Governance refers to all processes of governing, the institutions, processes, and practices through which issues of common concern are decided upon and regulated (*About good governance,* n.d.). Good governance can be defined as the degree to which each principle of governance is being followed and understood. According to the human rights council, the key attributes of good governance are but are not limited to, transparency, responsibility, accountability, participation, and responsiveness. True good governance is based on how well a government is performing and if they're maintaining the promises of the people regarding human rights. In this case, the channel of communication and power is bottom-up, the government must deliver based on the wishes of the people, otherwise, they're not living up to expectations. Simply put, good governance is if the government delivers on its promises, regarding issues stemming from the general public.

Good governance and human rights are mutually reinforcing (*About good governance*, n.d.). Governments require the standards and principles of human rights to guide them in making government decisions. One can view the human rights standards and principles as input, and the government decisions and policies as the output. The two essentially go hand in hand, one needs the other, and vice versa. Without good governance, human rights reforms have no credibility, but without human rights reforms, the government has poor input in deciding the proper courses of action and the decisions for policies they introduce. With that being said, a government must be free from corruption when responding to the requests of its people. As seen in many parts of the world, governments tend to ignore the wishes of their people in exchange for personal gain. This can be seen in many developing countries, which often leads to poor democracy. This relates to the idea of a pseudo-democracy. A country will describe its political system as a democracy but never offer a real choice for its citizens. Not only is this an example of corruption but it's also very unethical and immoral. Therefore, to work perfectly in unison, certain frameworks must be laid out for good governance to become a reality.

The links between good governance and human rights can be organized around four areas: democratic institutions, public service delivery, rule of law, and anti-corruption (*About good governance,* n.d.). Firstly, democratic institutions allow the public to participate in policy making, which values transparency, one of the most important attributes of good governance. Secondly, public service delivery is similar to democratic institutions regarding accountability and transparency. This area is important in upholding public participation in the government and gives human rights reforms and initiatives the spotlight. This also underlines the importance of transparency and accountability in good governance. The third area is the rule of law. Human rights initiatives and reforms are given the ability to create a national legal framework and power to implement that in legislation. Lastly, anti-corruption and fighting corruption within the government. This area essentially highlights the importance of transparency, accountability, and participation. Preventing and monitoring corruption is essential in good governance. This can be done by creating mechanisms for information sharing and monitoring how government decisions and policies are being made concerning public opinion. All of these factors play a role in facilitating good governance and fighting corruption within a government. One of the most important features of a perfect democracy is transparency. The public is obligated to know what goes on behind closed doors. It maintains a solid and healthy relationship with the government and its people. In return, the government acts on the wishes of the people and ultimately upholds human rights.

References

Human Rights Watch. Africa: Prioritize Education to Safeguard Children's Rights. (2021). Retrieved from https://www.hrw.org/news/2021/06/16/africa-prioritize-education-safeguard-childrens-rights

International Service for Human Rights. Who are human rights defenders? Retrieved from https://ishr.ch/about-human-rights/who-are-human-rights-defenders/

Mosher, C. F., Chapman, B. Edward, C. P. (n.d.). Public Administration. *Britannica*. Retrieved from https://www.britannica.com/topic/public-administration

Populism Studies. Pseudo Democracy. (n.d.). Retrieved from https://www.populismstudies.org/Vocabulary/pseudo-democracy/

Sustain Your Style. Inhumane working conditions. (n.d.). Retrieved from https://www.sustainyourstyle.org/en/working-conditions#:~:text=Employees%20usually%20work%20with%20no,-face%20verbal%20and%20 physical%20abuse.

Wegrich, K. (n.d.). Public Sector. Britannica. Retrieved from https://www.britannica.com/topic/public-sector

World Health Organization. Human Rights. (2022). Retrieved from https://www.who.int/news-room/fact-sheets/detail/human-rights-and-health#:~:text=The%20right%20to%20health%20must,based%20 approaches%20 is%20 meaningful%20 participation.

UNICEF. Child Labour. (n.d.). Retrieved from https://www.unicef.org/protection/child-labour

United Nations. About good governance. Retrieved from https://www.ohchr.org/en/good-governance/about-good-governance

Chapter 6: Human Rights and the Military

Aamna Aftab

Introduction

Human rights are an essential aspect of a well-ordered and civilized society. They form the backbone of the democratic and free world and provide a foundation for the protection of individual liberty and equality. Human rights are basic rights that every person has. Morally, these rights are not governed by the state because every human has a right to human rights. These can include the right to life, education, speech, religion, conscience, and thought – the list is endless. Though these basic rights *should* be available to all humans across the world, in many places, people are still fighting for their human rights. This chapter will cover multiple topics, solely focusing on human rights within the military, and how, at times, certain situations can cause difficulty for military forces to protect the human rights of civilians and non-combatants. This chapter aims to shed light on the challenges faced by military forces in protecting human rights. By exploring these issues, the reader will be able to broaden their understanding of the relationship between human rights and the military and highlight the critical importance of protecting human rights in all military operations.

Rules of Engagement

The Rules of Engagement (ROE) play a crucial role in controlling and managing the use of military force during armed conflict to protect the human rights of non-combatants and civilians. It dictates a set of rules such as who can use force and under what situation is it permissible. The content of ROE can vary according to context and the legal framework that applies to the situation. However, the fundamental guidelines of ROE include factors such as the following. Firstly, necessity. To achieve the military objective, the necessity of the use of force should be considered in a way that surpasses the expected harm to non-combatants and civilians. This ties into the second point, which is proportionality – the use of force should be limited in a way that it is proportional to the threat the military personnel is facing (United States Marine Corps, n.d.). With that said, it is against the ROE guidelines to abuse the use of military force by using it excessively. In terms of human rights, the military must respect the basic human rights of all non-combatants and refrain from committing acts that may constitute the use of military power in an abusive way.

Military Ethics and Human Rights

When in practice, at times, military forces may engage in activities that breach and violate human rights. This can range from unjustified displacement and arrest of civilians to torture and extrajudicial killing. Military ethics explores concepts such as the conduct of war, and decisions on when it is appropriate to engage in military operations. The role of human rights is to ensure actions are being done morally and ethically and to help military forces distinguish between right and wrong, especially during points when the law is not helpful (Emonet, 2018). It is imperative to understand military ethics and human rights because it is the sole duty of military forces to protect human rights under all circumstances. Military forces use a set of rules called the International Humanitarian law (IHL) to limit the effects of armed conflict (ICRC, n.d.). Note that the IHL can only be applied to armed conflict. The IHL is a crucial part of military ethics and human rights for many reasons. The IHL covers the protection of veterans, civilians, medical religious personnel, and those who are no longer taking a part in the fighting (ICRC, n.d.). The IHL also provides welfare restriction, which includes weapons and methods of welfare such as military tactics (ICRC, n.d.). Prisoners of war and other detained individuals are provided with the basic rights of protection and access to medical care. In other words, the main goal of the IHL is to ensure the protection of non-combatants and civilians and to minimize human suffering. This is done by the provision of a legal framework that is used during armed conflict.

Code of Conduct for Military Personnel

The code of conduct for military personnel varies across countries and different branches of service. However, a regular code of conduct outlines the ethical and professional standards for those serving in the military. For instance, in Canada the code of conduct is called "the statement of defence ethics" and it consists of six ethical obligations: integrity, loyalty, fairness, honesty, courage, and responsibility (Government of Canada, 2019). Human rights and the code of conduct for military personnel go hand in hand. The code of conduct for military personnel upholds a moral obligation to set laws that ensure that human rights are protected and respected. With that, the lives of civilians and non-combatants are protected as well. The code of conduct can also outline that prisoners of war need to be treated humanely – protecting them from harm and providing them with the necessary medical needs. The code of conduct for military personnel helps in the prevention of inhumane acts by military personnel. This includes acts such as torture, misuse of military power, or other forms of wrongful treatment against civilians and non-combatants.

Human Rights in Times of Conflict

During times when there is conflict in the military, human rights can become a critical concern. Many issues can arise, and many obstacles can come in the way of preserving human rights during times of conflict, which can cause difficulty in protecting human rights. One way in which human rights can be at risk during armed conflict includes during extrajudicial killing and torture. During times of conflict, there can be instances in which laws and the code of conduct for military personnel go unnoticed. When this happens, human rights are breached – the right to life comes with a violation. Armed conflict can also cause the loss of proper housing due to forced displacement or migration. The right to proper shelter and housing is a human right, and being forced out of this environment is a strong infringement on one's human rights. This can happen through physical force, which may include the use of violence, or through the use of verbally intimidating and causing fear in the civilians. Furthermore, the use of gunfire can cause a risk to what is considered a safe space for civilians, such as homes, schools, and hospitals. Moreover, in certain situations, restrictions on the freedom of expression can be implemented for reasons such as maintaining law, order, and control. This takes away the factor of free speech from civilians. Following the International Humanitarian Law, which is meant to protect the human rights of civilians and non-combatants, at times during the conflict, it ceases to provide individuals with basic protection of human rights.

Violation of Human Rights under The International Humanitarian Law (IHL)

A military base located in Guantanamo Bay, U.S. is a facility in which the IHL was breached and human rights were violated. The U.S. government implemented a detention facility, followed after the September 11th attacks, to hold suspected terrorists and enemy combatants as prisoners (OHCHR, 2022). However, it was discovered that the detained individuals were being tortured and treated poorly, which strongly constitutes an infringement upon human rights. This operation stained the U.S. government facility as an "unparalleled notoriety" site, as it strongly went against the United States rule of law (OHCHR, 2022). Many practices conducted at Guantanamo Bay constituted a violation of the IHL, which resulted in a violation of human rights due to the mistreatment of the detained. One of the practices conducted at this military base includes the use of enhanced interrogation techniques, which constituted a violation of the IHL and the law of human rights. Guantanamo Bay's enhanced interrogation techniques were more than simply having a conversation. One of the tactics used includes waterboarding, which is used to create a drowning sensation by pouring water over the individual's face as they are strapped somewhere which keeps the individual from moving. Threats of violence were also used by Guantanamo Bay during interrogations, in which the threats were as severe as threatening the detained individual with death or injury either upon them or their families. A tactic of sleep-depriving the detainee was also used. This is where detainees were forced to stay awake for an extenuating amount of hours, and days. Detainees were also forced to be in physically uncomfortable positions for elongated periods in an attempt to cause psychological and physical exhaustion. Sensory deprivation was also used, where the detainees had to stay in a dark room for a prolonged amount of time or were simply blindfolded for a long period. These tactics were used simply to retain pieces of information from the detainees. These tactics all go to prove that the IHL was not only violated in practice, but the Guantanamo Bay facility strongly infringed on human rights in more ways than one.

Military Personnel Rights

Just like every other civilian, military personnel deserve basic human rights. Military personnel also withhold unique rights and responsibilities that come with their military service. These range from multiple aspects, discussed in this sub-section. All military personnel is entitled to basic human rights, such as the right to life. Every human being has the right to life, and no level of authority has the right to make a violation in this matter. All military personnel is entitled to protection from harm and extrajudicial killing – the unlawful and unjustified killing of another person on behalf of the state without any legal consultation. Though this does not mean that removing the right to life with legal consultation is correct, without it, it is simply considered an arbitrary deprivation of life, which occurs during military conflicts. Extrajudicial killing by itself is an infringement on human rights, thus leading to war crimes, as it targets non-combatants, civilians, and other innocent lives. Extrajudicial killing is considered a war crime especially when it is committed as part of a systematic attack against civilians and non-combatants. Not only does it put innocent lives at risk, but it causes individuals to forcefully flee from their homes.

Along with the protection of human rights, military personnel has unique rights and responsibilities, designed to ensure that they can carry out their duties in a manner in which human rights are protected along the way. During the military conflict, soldiers will undergo tough situations in which lethal force may be used to protect themselves, resulting in necessity. This is where force is used to achieve an objective while protecting civilians from harm, which is an example of the protection of human rights, and a military personnel's unique responsibility. This is just one example of human rights and the rights and responsibilities of military personnel, but the list goes on – the freedom of expression, the right to fair treatment, privacy, and the right to refuse unlawful orders. Military personnel hold the same human rights as every other individual, however, as military personnel, they have to protect these rights not only for themselves but for civilians and non-combatants as well.

The Impact of Military Actions on Civilian Populations

The actions of the military both during armed conflict and in the aftermath can have an impact on the human rights of civilians. One of the most significant impacts of military actions is civilian casualties. During times of conflict, the lives of civilians are at huge risk, leading to injury or death. Many military authorities use weapons and explosives to defeat the opposition, however, these deadly tools can strongly bring harm to civilians as well. This can all cause significant injury and death during battle, and the aftermath can lead to permanent mental and physical injuries for the survivors. It is the responsibility of military personnel to protect the lives, the human rights, of civilians – however, more often than not, during battle, military actions negatively affect the lives of civilians and non-combatants. Furthermore, another consequence of armed conflict in the military includes the displacement and forced migration of civilians.

This is a strong violation of human rights, as it takes away many basic human rights such as the right to adequate housing, the right to education, and many other basic needs. It is a fundamental principle of International Humanitarian Law to protect the human rights of civilians. In a situation like this, the military has a responsibility to provide those suffering from displacement with humanitarian aid to ensure that civilians have access to basic human needs such as health care, education, food, and shelter. Military forces need to ensure that civilians are being kept away from harm, and they have a responsibility to protect things such as their homes and hospitals. All in all, the impact of military actions on the civilian population can strongly impact human rights. Hence, it is essential to make sure to protect these rights during times of conflict to avoid negative effects on
civilians and combatants.

The Role of the Military in Promoting Human Rights

There are multiple ways in which the military can play a positive role in promoting and protecting human rights, both domestically and internationally. The military has a critical responsibility to uphold the rule of law. This ensures that all civilians are treated equally and fairly, and their rights are protected. By enforcing the rule of law and making sure that laws are enforced, the military forces can strongly help to promote the importance of human rights. Not only that, but this also helps to create a culture of respect for human rights. The military can also play a positive role in promoting and protecting human rights through peacekeeping operations. This is used to regulate human rights by providing protection to civilians in areas affected by conflict, supporting the reintegration of former combatants, providing security, and regulating the rule of law (Better World Campaign, 2023).

The military can promote human rights in disaster relief efforts as well. This can be done by ensuring that humanitarian aid is distributed in a fair manner based on need instead of political factors. Furthermore, by protecting disaster victims, the military can promote and protect their human rights. This can be done by providing security and protection from violence, and ensuring civilians have access to basic human needs such as food and shelter. The military can promote a sustainable recovery by working with local communities to support recovery efforts, such as the restoration of infrastructure. This will create a secure environment for civilians and will promote and protect human rights.

Arbitrary Detention Use by Military Forces

Many issues can occur in how a military force uses its power, both in the context of armed conflict, as well as in other situations. Human rights are infringed upon in many ways through mistreatment by military forces, which will be discussed in this section. Starting with arbitrary detention – is a strong violation of human rights that occurs through torture and mistreatment conducted by military forces. This constitutes arrests and detention given by the military forces without any legal justification. It happens purely on a bias and can occur for reasons such as political beliefs, and racial, ethnic, and cultural differences.

Arbitrary detention can have a strong psychological and physical effect on the detainee, as torture and mistreatment are used by military forces. Though this practice has been banned by International Humanitarian Law, it continues to occur in multiple places throughout the world. For example, the US military detention camps located in Guantanamo Bay, in which detainees are kept captive for several years without being charged for anything. The detention camp was discussed earlier in the paper under the International Humanitarian Law section. The use of torture and mistreatment is an unacceptable issue, especially since there are laws that strictly prohibit forms of mistreatment such as arbitrary detention. This topic continues to be a complex issue because to this day, human rights are at risk by military forces, hence this issue should be strongly addressed.

Military Justice System and Upholding Human Rights

The foremost priority of the military justice system is to uphold and protect human rights. The military justice system ensures human rights of civilians and military personnel are not violated. However, there are often many challenges that come with ensuring the military justice system deals with this matter in a fair and unbiased manner, while ensuring the rule of law is being abided by. The military justice system must operate without any influence from external factors. Military courts can strongly uphold human rights if they work independently – however, they should be subject to the same legal procedures and standards as supreme courts. The military justice system can face challenges in upholding human rights if they receive some sort of influence from the military chain of command. This can result in the undermining of the court's impartiality. It causes a violation of human rights, causing difficulties and inconsistencies in the military justice system in the future.

Similar to civilian supreme courts across countries, the military courts have the duty of enforcing the right to a fair trial to uphold human rights, ensuring the protection of human rights. Without the right to a fair trial, the violations committed against human rights would be left unpunished, causing the military justice system to repeatedly lack accountability and a fair trial (Equality and Human Rights Commission, n.d.). The military justice system has the unquestionable responsibility of protecting human rights – without this, decisions made in court would be unjust, and the military justice system would fail in upholding the human rights of military personnel and civilians. The military justice system has to follow the same legal standards as national courts to ensure human rights are being protected, not only under the military justice system but the constitution of the country as well.

References

Emonet, M. F. (2018, November 16). The importance of ethics education in military training. Army University Press. Retrieved from https://www.armyupress.army.mil/Journals/NCO-Journal/Archives/2018/November/Ethics/#:~:text=Military%20ethics%2C%20like%20medical%20or,laws%20are%20no%20longer%20helpful

Equality and Human Rights Commission. (n.d.). Article 6 - Right to a fair trial. Retrieved from https://www.equalityhumanrights.com/en/human-rights-act/article-6-right-fair-trial

Government of Canada. (2019, June 18). The Statement of Defence Ethics. Canada. Retrieved from https://www.canada.ca/en/department-national-defence/corporate/reports-publications/fundamentals-canadian-defence-ethics/statement-of-defence-ethics.html

ICRC. (n.d.). What is international humanitarian law? Advisory Service on International Humanitarian Law. Retrieved from https://www.icrc.org/en/doc/assets/files/other/what_is_ihl.pdf

Office of The High Commissioner. (2022, January 10). Guantanamo Bay: "Ugly chapter of unrelenting human rights violations" – UN experts. OHCHR. Retrieved from https://www.ohchr.org/en/press-releases/2022/01/guantanamo-bay-ugly-chapter-unrelenting-human-rights-violations-un-experts#:~:text=%E2%80%9C-Guantanamo%20Bay%20is%20a%20site,of%20their%20most%20fundamental%20rights.%E2%80%9D

United States Marine Corps. (n.d.). Law of War/Introduction to Rules of Engagement. Retrieved from https://www.trngcmd.marines.mil/Portals/207/Docs/TBS/B130936%20Law%20of%20War%20and%20Rules%20Of%20Engagement.pdf

UN Peacekeeping. Better World Campaign. (2023, January 12). Retrieved from https://betterworldcampaign.org/un-peacekeeping#:~:text=Today's%20peacekeeping%20operations%20are%20called,organizing%20elections%2C%20protecting%20and%20promoting

Chapter 7: Human Rights and the Police

Madiha Ansari

Introduction

Since the 18th century, human rights and their inclusion in several aspects of the world's history have raised several controversies and debates. Due to the long history of human rights, political and legal development has changed and adapted consistently (Wright, 2016). Although the topic of human rights is crucial, many philosophers argued about the concept of natural rights that human beings possess. For instance, the "natural" human right to have access to basic human needs (Wright, 2016).

During the 20th century, human rights were extensively violated, which caused authorities to take action to secure the notion of human rights. For example, after the events of World War II, the United Nations (UN) took major steps to fight the conflict arising during the cold-war period. In 1948, the UN Universal Declaration on Human Rights was established (Wright, 2016). Not long after, in 1963, another UN conference was held which allowed a human rights standard to be set internationally. This conference was based on the "Role of the Police in the Protection of Human Rights" (Martin, 2021). Many different treaties and codes of conduct were introduced to train and inspect police officers. The laws and regulations regarding the framework of human rights have helped policymakers and authorities to implement projects in many different countries (Martin, 2021). These steps are taken to reform police forces in countries such as Ireland, where post-conflict issues have consistently occurred, while also improving police forces and ethics in countries such as America and Canada, where policing has become controversial (Martin, 2021).

It is necessary to consider that despite the inclusion of the Human Rights Act in 1998, and several conferences aimed to resolve the issues of human rights and policing, many police officers do not comply with the rules and ethical training. For these reasons, there has been a rise in research regarding police brutality, racism in police officers, discriminatory police activities, and risks to public health (Wright, 2016). However, these actions are not newly introduced. There have been many instances in the past where police officers have violated human rights and the Articles of Convention under the Human Rights Act 1998. The Articles of Convention, which will be discussed later in this chapter, mention the human rights, rules, and laws that police officers and authorities must follow (Wright, 2016). Violation of these acts results in a lack of public trust in police, suspension/revoking of one's police license, and detailed investigation of the police officer involved in breaking the law (Wright, 2016).

Police Ethics & Human Rights

Law enforcement personnel, such as police officers, face many challenges when performing their duty. Apart from physical exhaustion, police officers are also confronted by moral and ethical decision-making at all times (Blumberg et al., 2020). Considering the importance of ethical decision-making, in the profession of policing, helps in understanding the additional fatigue that police officers experience. There are many instances where police either face an emotional difficulty or engage in an unlawful activity; both due to the burden of moral risks that they must take (Blumberg et al., 2020). For example, police officers may disagree with certain beliefs and rules that their supervisors have ordered them to follow, due to their morals and ethics. However, since it is necessary to follow the organization's policies, police officers experience moral distress and ethical exhaustion. Therefore, this concept has been phrased as "the cost of caring" (Blumberg et al., 2020).

On the other hand, unethical decision-making, due to the burden and responsibility of making morally and ethically correct decisions, leads to numerous problems and misconduct. As the saying goes "with great power comes great responsibility", police officers have the power to decide how they treat an individual, whether it is a criminal or an innocent person. Based on that reason, it is expected that police officers' manners and behaviour follow ethically accepted norms and values since the police are present to help and secure the public (Blumberg et al., 2020). According to research, emotional and ethical exhaustion in police officers leads to depression and anxiety. Furthermore, in another research, a relationship was found between anxiety and unethical decision-making. Although it is not explicitly researched on police officers, the possibility of anxiety and depression being the cause of unethical behaviour is a topic to be discovered and considered (Blumberg et al., 2020).

With the increase in newspaper articles and research regarding police misconduct and unethical behaviour toward civilians, it has become important to remind law enforcement and authorities about human rights. One of the primary duties of a police officer is to provide a safe and secure environment for the society. Police authorities and organizations exist to develop and strengthen the social and economic components of society, by acting as a public service (Țical, 2017). Unfortunately, as mentioned previously, not all police officers abide by the rules of law and code of conduct. Policing in minority communities has always been alleged to mistreat individuals worldwide. Harassment, one's death while in police custody, and failure to fight against criminal activities are some of the examples by which police mistreat minority communities (Neyroud & Beckley, 2001).

Moreover, there have been cases where police officers have violated the Articles of Convention. One of the examples includes the case of *Osman v UK* (1998) where the police were found to be neglecting criminal case investigation (Wright, 2016). This case demonstrated the violation of *Article 6* which refers to a human's right to a fair trial. Other instances include the violation of *Article 8* which talks about the human right to privacy. In cases such as *Malone v UK* (1984) and *Kruslin v France* (1990), a lack of legal regulation among police organizations was found. A breach of privacy occurred for the individuals involved in the case, where police monitored phone calls without a proper procedure, warrant, or verdict (Wright, 2016).

Code of Conduct for Police Personnel

Code of Conduct for law enforcement personnel exists all over the world. Most countries have similar Codes of Conduct for police personnel to ensure fair treatment of the public. Since police officers are meant to perform as public service workers, there are several rules and regulations that they must follow to perform to the best of their abilities. According to the Code of Conduct in Canada, the Royal Canadian Mounted Police (RCMP) emphasizes the importance of avoiding discrimination and harassment within the police force and in society (Government of Canada, 2014). Since there is also an influence of the Canadian Charter of Rights and Freedoms in Canada, the RCMP is strict on respecting the rights of all individuals and stating that one does not "compromise or abuse their authority, power or position" (Government of Canada, 2014).

In Ontario, Canada specifically, the Code of Conduct explicitly states that a police officer is prohibited from treating another person in a manner that would contravene the Human Rights Code or the Canadian Charter of Rights and Freedoms. Some of the examples, when interacting with the public, include police officers should not make an arrest knowing that the specific arrest is unlawful, they should not authorize any physical or psychological harm when it is deemed unlawful, and if an individual is under the police custody, it is necessary for police officials to ensure their security and safety at all times (Ontario Regulation, 2019). Furthermore, the Code of Conduct also specifies that a police officer has committed misconduct if they treat people unfairly with discrimination against race, sex, ethnicity, and so on. Additionally, any use of abusive language, profanities, assaults, unlawful acts, and inappropriate physical harassment, comes under the section of committing misconduct (Ontario.ca, 2020). Code of Conduct, under the Ontario regulations, also states that insubordination, neglecting one's duties, being deceitful, breaching of confidential information and privacy, corrupt practices, and unnecessary utilization of authority, will result in severe consequences in which the police officer can be charged and punished for rebelling against the Code of Conduct (Ontario.ca, 2020).

In the UK, most, if not all, similar practices are followed. Honesty, integrity, respect, and equality are the basic Codes of Conduct that police officers are required to follow. In addition, they are also required to follow lawful instructions and make ethical decisions, which includes reporting any misbehaviour and improper conduct performed by their fellow peer(s) or colleague(s) (legislation.gov.uk, 2008). Despite the similarities and differences between the Codes of Conduct for police officers in various countries, most countries also abide by the rules set by the UN. The Code of Conduct for Law Enforcement Officials was adopted in 1979 by the General Assembly Resolution. A set of 8 Articles were introduced that law enforcement personnel are required to follow (United Nations, 2023).

Some of the examples of the various Articles are as follows: Article 1 states that law enforcement officials should always fulfil their lawful duties, serve their communities, and protect the public from illegal activities. Article 2 emphasizes the respect and protection a police officer should provide to the public while upholding people's human rights and dignity. Article 3 allows law enforcement officials to use force against an individual, within limits, but only when lawfully necessary. Article 4 strictly prohibits police officers to share confidential information unless it is needed for justifiable reasons. Article 5 states that law enforcement officials are strictly ordered to not use any inhumane, degrading, torturous, or cruel treatment or punishment against other individuals (United Nations, 2023). Therefore, the police Code of Conduct is extremely strict and specific in addressing the protection of human rights.

Police Use of Force and Human Rights

Despite the strict police Code of Conduct, some law enforcements have, and continue to, act against the conduct that is required to be followed. Based on those reasons, the police use of force (UOF) has become a highly researched topic during the past few years. As mentioned previously in this chapter, police officers are not allowed to UOF without any significant reason, transparency, or accountability for the specific action. Therefore, to protect human rights and ensure the safety of humans, law enforcement must make decisions for UOF by taking responsibility and being willing to take accountability for their actions (Basu, 2022). One of the main points to consider is that UOF does not only account for taking an action, it also includes not taking an action. Looking into historical events, law enforcement has been impacted politically as well as through societal pressure to either under-react or over-react when making hard policing decisions against a certain community or individual. An example of this is the under-reaction of the German police when the Nazi genocide occurred in World War II (Basu, 2022).

Some of the cases, where police UOF was used inappropriately or not in the correct manner, happened due to the lack of police force involved. Lack of trust and confidence in the police increased since the police officers did not take action to prevent a crime from happening, such as the murder of Stephen Lawrence in 1993, a young British black man, who died due to the absence of support from the police for the black community. Therefore, the black community lost their sense of security with the police and claimed them to be institutionally racist (Basu, 2022). Since human rights are bound to be protected by law enforcement, it is important for police forces to gain the trust and confidence of the public for them to take appropriate actions and use the ideal level of force based on public consent. It is suggested that police officers are recruited based on their EQ and IQ so that crime can be dealt with more wisely and fairly. In addition, police officers are encouraged to engage with their community and neighbourhoods for them to get a better understanding, insight, and connection with the people they have vowed to protect (Basu, 2022).

One of the main issues in police UOF is that there is no specific standard on how police officers' UOF is trained and evaluated. Although certain decisions, made by the police, can be objectively measured, such as the accuracy of shooting/not shooting decision, other behaviours require a subjective measure, dependent on the police officer who is making a decision, for example, situation awareness (Di Nota et al., 2021). By conducting a study on this matter, researchers found that objective decision-making was consistent whereas the subjective measures varied. This is because there are no set criteria for when a police officer should pull the trigger or use any other type of force. The decision rests solely on the police officer responsible and present at the moment (Di Nota et al., 2021). Therefore, based on the study, it was recommended that police officers should be trained by taking into account both subjective and objective matters. In all stages of training, it should be mandatory for police officers to not only have a better understanding of when to use force/when to not use force but also have an awareness of the situation they are in, and then make an appropriate decision by taking all factors into account (Di Nota et al., 2021).

Along with appropriate training, law enforcement must revise the importance of human rights. As mentioned previously, police organizations exist to protect and secure the public from any harm or criminal activity. However, if the same individuals, who are protecting the community, become a threat to public safety, then extreme measures, to revive the ethical and best practices, are necessary to be taken. One of the models presented, to decrease the unjust, unfair, and disrespectful UOF from the police against the public, is called the procedural justice model of policing (Wood et al., 2020). In this model, any UOF by a police officer needs to be justified through transparency, explanation of a certain action, taking responsibility for the act committed and responding to any criticism or concerns of the community. Studies have shown that by receiving correct and ethical training, police officers' behaviour has significantly improved when on the field or on duty. Along with having the pressure of accountability, considering and reminding oneself about the weight of human rights and public protection, police officers are much more likely to act fairly and respectfully towards civilians, and use appropriate UOF (Wood et al., 2020).

Human Rights and Police Accountability

Having the responsibility of human life and security as one of the main components, police officers inevitably hold accountability for several actions that are either committed by others or themselves. For example, an increase in the crime rate or police brutality, both fall under police accountability. Furthermore, public health and justice are also additional tasks that police officers are responsible for. In Canada, the police have become one of the main responders to health concerns and socioeconomic issues in the community. Therefore, the police constantly have interactions with individuals who use drugs or have mental health issues, harming those specific people (Butler et al., 2022). Police accountability mustn't reach a level where there is a system failure - in which the police are held accountable for situations that are not in their area of expertise. A person experiencing a mental health issue or substance abuse problem is out of the control of police officers. These situations require a separate organization or facility, such as health care services, that can be contacted instead of the police (Butler et al., 2022). Although taking care of the public's health is one of the duties of police officers, they should

Introduction to Ethics and Human Rights 93

not be held accountable or blamed for disrespecting human rights when the situation is not in their job description or
Code of Conduct.

However, when the situation is under the police officers' expertise and responsibility, the public has criticized them for not taking appropriate actions and decisions. In the United States, police brutality has become an ongoing issue that directly targets human rights and safety. As mentioned previously, some cases have had involvement of under-reaction of the police. On the other hand, in other cases, there has been an overreaction of police officers. For example, the case of Michael Brown, a black unarmed teenager who was shot by the police, led to a revival among the public to debate discriminatory practices of the police as well as police brutality against certain ethnicities/races (McGregor, 2015). Along with that, the infamous case of George Floyd, a black individual who was murdered by the police, started a Black Lives Matter movement to highlight the mistrust between the community and the police and the misconduct of the police against human lives and rights (Goulka et al., 2021). These cases fall under the accountability of the police force. Due to the severity of the situation, many people began to favour the decision of defunding the police and limiting the authority that the police holds. This demonstrates that along with the public, law enforcement is also negatively impacted. Hence, it is important to hold police officers accountable for their actions and decision-making.

Public health and safety are compromised when human rights are not respected by the police (Goulka et al., 2021). When criminal activity occurs, it is up to law enforcement to fight crime and take justified decisions. More often than not, the decision and the situation are extremely difficult to judge but that is why police officers hold major responsibilities and authority in the community. For the public to respect the power and role of police officers, then police officers are also required to respect human rights. Thus, improving police-community relations, modifying the training process by using real-life scenarios, and educating the police as well as the public about human rights will increase the trust between the public and the police (McGregor, 2015).

Furthermore, the burden of accountability and fear of taking the wrong step will decrease since law enforcement will be made more aware of human rights and how important it is to respect and know one's responsibility.

References:

Basu, N. (2022). Maintaining Confidence in Police Use of Force in Western Liberal Democracies. *Cambridge Journal of Evidence-Based Policing, 6*(3-4), 69–82. doi: 10.1007/s41887-022-00076-9

Blumberg, D. M., Papazoglou, K., & Schlosser, M. D. (2020). Organizational Solutions to the Moral Risks of Policing. *International Journal of Environmental Research and Public Health, 17*(20), 7461. doi: 10.3390/ijerph17207461

Butler, A., Zakimi, N., & Greer, A. (2022). Total systems failure: police officers' perspectives on the impacts of the justice, health, and social service systems on people who use drugs. *Harm Reduction Journal, 19*(1). doi: 10.1186/s12954-022-00629-1

Di Nota, P. M., Chan, J. F., Huhta, J.-M., & Andersen, J. P. (2021). Considering Objective and Subjective Measures for Police Use of Force Evaluation. *International Journal of Environmental Research and Public Health, 18*(10), 5351. doi: 10.3390/ijerph18105351

Goulka, J., Del Pozo, B., & Beletsky, L. (2021). From public safety to public health: Re-envisioning the goals and methods of policing. *Journal of Community Safety and Well-Being, 6*(1), 22–27. doi: 10.35502/jcswb.184

Government of Canada: Legislative Services Branch. (2014). *Royal Canadian Mounted Police Regulations, 2014.* Justice.gc.ca. Retrieved from https://laws.justice.gc.ca/eng/regulations/SOR-2014-281/page-5.html#h-808732

Legislation.gov.uk. (2008). *The Police (Conduct) Regulations 2008*. Retrieved from https://www.legislation.gov.uk/uksi/2008/2864/schedule/made

Martin, R. (2021). Righting the Police: How do Officers Make Sense of Human Rights? *The British Journal of Criminology*, *62*(3), 551–567. doi: 10.1093/bjc/azab067

McGregor, A. (2015). Politics, Police Accountability, and Public Health: Civilian Review in Newark, New Jersey. *Journal of Urban Health*, *93*(S1), 141–153. doi: 10.1007/s11524-015-9998-4

Neyroud, P., & Beckley, A. (2001). *Policing, Ethics, and Human Rights*. Willan. doi: 10.4324/9781843924678

Ontario Regulation. (2019). *Consultation Draft*. Retrieved from https://www.ontariocanada.com/registry/showAttachment.do?postingId=36948&attachmentId=49358

Ontario.ca. (2014). *Law Document English View*. Retrieved from https://www.ontario.ca/laws/regulation/100268#BK39

Țical, G. (2017). *Ethics of the Police Profession and Respecting the Human Rights*. Ssrn.com. Retrieved from https://papers.ssrn.com/sol3/papers.cfm?abstract_id=3521180

United Nations. (2023). *Code of Conduct for Law Enforcement Officials*. OHCHR. Retrieved from https://www.ohchr.org/en/instruments-mechanisms/instruments/code-conduct-law-enforcement-officials

Wood, G., Tyler, T. R., & Papachristos, A. V. (2020). Procedural justice training reduces police use of force and complaints against officers. *Proceedings of the National Academy of Sciences*, *117*(18), 9815–9821. doi: 10.1073/pnas.1920671117

Wright, A. (2000). An Introduction to Human Rights and Policing. *The Police Journal, 73*(3), 193–209. doi: 10.1177/0032258X0007300302

Chapter 8: Human Rights and the Judiciary

Brianna Bedran

In this chapter, we will be looking into how human rights laws are enforced, how the courts interpret and produce these laws that have progressed over time, as well what happens in the case that controversies arise with countries following these laws. We will find by the end of this chapter that while there is a common notion of human rights in the western world and reflected by legislation such as the international human rights laws produced by the UN it is not always the case that these rights fit every society. This can influence human rights laws and the courts' implementation of such laws even with legislative power.

How are Human Rights Enforced

International human rights legislations include within the document the requirements of nation's governments to either act in specific ways or these legislations can even specify to refrain from certain actions. These laws are implemented to protect and advocate for human rights as well as the fundamental freedoms of individuals or groups (United Nations, 2023). We can contribute these guidelines to one of the great achievements of human rights history: the United Nations and the implementation of this inclusive and comprehensive body of human rights law. The international human rights laws are a "universal and internationally protected code to which all nations can subscribe and all people aspire", as stated by the UN (United Nations, 2023).

The foundations of this body of law can be found within the Charter of the United Nations as well as the Universal Declaration of Human Rights, which was adopted by the General Assembly in 1945 and 1948. Respectively, these international human rights laws have for a long time now been acknowledged as the international body of law for human rights and have made significant improvements since its first development (United Nations, 2023) Hence, the implementation of such laws has provided civilians with the critical protection against any potential unlawful government action as any acts committed that do not abide by the bounds of this legislation are subject to investigation. The United Nations has defined a broad range of internationally accepted rights, including civil, cultural, economic, political, and social rights. These rights have further established mechanisms to promote and protect these rights and to aid states in carrying out their responsibilities when it comes to human rights (United Nations, 2023).

A series of international human rights treaties and other instruments adopted since the first establishment of international human rights laws in 1945 have bestowed legal forms on inherent human rights and developed the body of international human rights (United Nations, 2023). However, other instruments have been adopted at the regional level of government as well, which reflect on the particular human rights concerns of that particular area and provide for specific mechanisms of protection for the demographic of the community (United Nations, 2023).

How Do Governments Follow the International Human Rights Law?

International human rights law lays down obligations that States are bound to respect. By becoming abiding parties to international treaties, States assume the obligations and duties under international law to respect, as well as to protect and fulfil such human rights (United Nations, 2023). For example, the obligation to respect means that States must refrain from interfering with or curtailing the enjoyment of human rights. Similarly, the obligation to protect requires States to protect individuals and groups against any potential human rights abuses done by the government or other individuals (United Nations, 2023). The obligation to fulfil defines that States must take on positive action to actively produce its citizens' enjoyment of basic human rights (United Nations, 2023) However, this obligation has raised controversy on the topic of human rights as different countries interpret inherit rights differently, which we will further look into in this chapter.

While the Universal Declaration of Human Rights has universal rights, local governments must adopt their own that provide even more relief for the particular demographic of their community. This is why typically, most states have also adopted their single constitutions and other laws which formally protect basic human rights inspired by the UN's interpretations (United Nations, 2023). Still, the Universal Declaration of Human Rights maintains that there are international treaties and customary laws that form the backbone of international human rights law. Other instruments, such as declarations, guidelines, and principles adopted at the international level also contribute to the understanding, implementation, and development of human rights laws (United Nations, 2023). At the very least, respect for human rights requires the establishment of the rule of law at the national and international levels (United Nations, 2023).

The Progression of Human Rights

As previously mentioned, over time these laws have been expanded and modified as our idea of human rights is always moving towards more inclusive policies. As social movements, organizations, and other advocates of human rights have helped shift traditional standards of civil liberties, this change is necessary and it also does not mean we ever have to stop anywhere when it comes to the progress of our ideas of human rights. Since the first implementation of the document, the United Nations has gradually over time further developed human rights law to encompass specific standards for more marginalized groups including women, children, persons with disabilities, minorities, and other vulnerable groups, who currently possess rights that protect them from discrimination that had long been common in many societies (United Nations, 2023). Without this change in legislation, the progress of human rights would never truly be acknowledged. Thankfully, the power and influence of social movements have contributed to this legislative change and will likely continue to do so. (cite) With the idea of rights constantly expanding, there will always be modifications to this legislation and new adjustments in the courtroom of interpreting rights. This does not mean any previous laws were bad, it is simply that ideally laws are adjusted to further expand their interpretation of protection and democracy.

Human Rights Laws in Canada

As noted in the second section of this chapter, countries can adopt their human rights laws under the guidelines of the Universal Declaration of Human Rights. We can look at an example of this type of adoption such as the Canadian Human Rights Act. The purpose of this Act as stated in the legislation is to broaden "the human rights laws in Canada to give effect, within the responsibility of matters coming within the legislative authority of Parliament, to the principle that all individuals should have an opportunity equal with other individuals to make for themselves the lives that they are able and wish to have and to have their needs accommodated, consistent with their duties and obligations as members of society" (Government of Canada, 2023). This done so "without being hindered in or prevented from doing so by discriminatory practices based on race, national or ethnic origin, colour, religion, age, sex, sexual orientation, gender identity or expression, marital status, family status, genetic characteristics, disability or conviction for an offence for which a pardon has been granted or in respect of which a record suspension has been ordered (Government of Canada, 2023). For all purposes of the Canadian Human Rights Act, the forbidden means of discrimination cover broadly cover a variety of grounds such as race, national or ethnic origin, colour, religion, age, sex, sexual orientation, gender identity or expression, marital status, family status, genetic characteristics, disability and conviction for an offence for which a pardon has been granted or in respect of which a record suspension has been ordered (Government of Canada, 2023). There is also the Charter of Rights and Freedoms which protects individuals from unlawful government action. The Canadian government declares that The Canadian Charter of Rights and Freedoms protects rights and freedoms, including freedom of expression and the right to equality. It forms part of the Canadian Constitution, which is the highest law in all of Canada and is classified as one of the country's greatest accomplishments. That is why every year on April 17, the nation celebrates the anniversary of the Charter which was signed in 1982 (Government of Canada, 2023).

Human Rights Laws and the Indigenous Community

It has been contested how indigenous peoples' right to land is quite similar to the right to non-discrimination in international law (United Nations, 2023). It is significant to address how Indigenous peoples have been classified as historically colonised subjects and the victims of land deprivation in international law.

As such, even though the right to land has been recognised as an established state practice, there are concerns regarding its incompatibility with the principle of substantive non-discrimination under international human rights law (United Nations, 2023). It is important to acknowledge how some groups are neglected in the draft of human rights, as even with all the progress made there is still room for improvement.

Improvements to address the needs of the indigenous community regarding human rights have been made, such as the UN drafting a separate document of the United Nations Declaration of the Rights of Indigenous People. In the document, it is declared that Indigenous peoples possess the right to the full enjoyment, as a collective and as well as individuals, of all human rights and the most fundamental freedoms as accepted in the Charter of the United Nations, the Universal Declaration of Human Rights and international human rights laws (United Nations, 2007). As such, Indigenous peoples and individuals are free and equal to any other non-Indigenous peoples and individuals and maintain the fundamental right to be free from any form of discrimination in the exercise of their rights. It is specified that this form of discrimination in particular based on their indigenous origin or identity (United Nations, 2007). Furthermore, Indigenous peoples have the right to self-determination. This is because this right may freely determine their political status and freely pursue their economic, social, and cultural development. Indigenous peoples, in exercising their right to self-determination, also possess the right to autonomy or self-government in matters relating to their internal and local affairs, as well as ways and means for financing their functions (United Nations, 2007).

Human Rights and the Courtroom

Unfortunately, discrimination can and has taken place in the courtroom, which is where one looks for the fair and impartial administration of the law, and it is particularly damaging. When there is a case of discriminatory law, the search for fairness is significantly compromised. Take for example a form of legislation that states women may not independently choose to travel, work outside the home, or undergo certain medical procedures without permission from male relatives. Just as concerning, and much more widespread than one would expect from the criminal justice system, is when judges' decisions are swayed by harmful gender stereotypes in their interpretation of the law and handing down of decisions (United Nations, 2023). This is most common in cases that are related to gender-based violence, the family, equal work opportunities, and women's sexual and reproductive health. Also, when judges make decisions based on harmful gender stereotypes, for example taking a woman's sexual life into account when deciding her legal rights and protection against rape or domestic violence, this is a human rights violation (United Nations, 2023). The UN addresses this type of human rights violations in the courtroom and this is why the UDHR and international laws are consistent to protect this form of discrimination.

Human Rights Laws in Non-Western Countries

It is not uncommon for states to go after two different and incompatible approaches to human rights when it comes to domestic and international affairs (Rahman, S., et al. 2022) As such, powerful states have often leaned towards interpreting international human rights norms according to their national interest, more than less powerful states (Rahman, S., et al. 2022). As an example, we will look into the case of human rights laws in China and how this can defer to traditional conceptions of human rights. First, let's take a look at why such disagreements can occur.

Human Rights Laws Controversy

It is difficult to implement any type of universal understanding of any concept with the difference of nations' cultures. As such, one of the most common and intense debates within the human rights community is the one pitting universalists against cultural relativists. Universalists believe that there should be an agreed understanding of the fundamental rights of any person regardless of demographics. Whereas the cultural relativism debate addresses how cultural distinction can rightfully influence western ideas of human rights (Ishay, 2004). While it is still relative to human rights discussion now, this debate, however, can be traced back to ancient times, when the popular historian Herodotus argued more than 2,000 years ago that there were no universal ethics (Ishay, 2004).

The central point of this argument is that cultural relativism is a repeated product of a historical failure to promote universal rights discourses in practice, instead of a legitimate alternative to the comprehensive vision offered by universalists' stand on democratic justice. The invocation of cultural rights most often occurs when a particular group feels deprived of political, social, and economic rights so easily enjoyed by others (Ishay, 2004). Attempts to fuse liberal and socialist perspectives on rights (first- and second-generation rights) into one Western philosophical tradition echo the current third-world supplication against Western cultural values, or what has been described in terms of 'the West versus the Rest' (Ishay, 2004). After hundreds of years of colonialism as well an accelerating globalisation process dominated by all things Western such as Western media, Western technology, Western values, and Western products, arguments favoured in terms of defending the alleged uniqueness of non-Western cultural traditions against Western values (or vice-versa), may seem almost pointless. That division is based on the assumption that Western values are associated largely with individual civil and political rights, whereas people in developing countries tend to emphasise rights related to the welfare of groups consistent with their cultural and religious traditions (Ishay, 2004).

Human Rights Laws in China

While there is global governance of human rights in the Western world, different countries outside of this region may interpret human rights differently based on their cultural values. This has proved true in the case of China's human rights laws. It is most generally acknowledged that China has had a complex, weary, and most often contentious dynamic with the idea of universal governance of human rights. A major factor in this troubling relationship is the generally weak, and now even further deteriorating, human rights record in domestic practices (Zhang et al., 2020). However, it is still also increasingly accepted that China is not just no longer a norm taker, it has also become growingly influential as well as aggressive in shaping its global normative order of human rights to ensure a better fit with China's own domestic and international preferences (Zhang et al., 2020). There is a further set of distinct contradictions in the relationship between China and the global human rights norms and regimes. On the one hand, China has been conditioned into signing and accepting most human rights treaties and conventions (Zhang et al., 2020). Hence, the human rights rhetoric is omnipresent in Chinese official discourse (Zhang et al., 2020). On the other hand, such ubiquity has not been matched by any form of improved record of political and civil rights in China. The approvals of international treaties have had only a limited, if not entirely negligible, impact on the human rights practices within China (Zhang et al., 2020). Its interpretation or attempt to alteration of international human rights will have an inclusive influence in a powerful state like China, unlike the less powerful states (Yongjin et al., 2020).

The states' double-standard diplomacy is a common and not-so-springing occurrence, however, China's double-standard practices in the area of international human rights are getting increasingly particularly significant due to its outstanding economic growth that has greatly improved its diplomatic clout, giving the nation room and means to rise to prominence in world affairs (Rahman, S., et al. 2022). In other words, it can be understood that China's every move at the international institutions is being noted and addressed worldwide and is open to receive criticism unlike the Western states as China has found its footing at the United Nations human rights bodies (Rahman, S., et al. 2022). There are all sorts of literature in light of states' behaviour on human rights violations and states implementing universal human rights norms subsist, including the contestation of state sovereignty and human rights regime (Rahman, S., et al. 2022. Yet, there has been very little documented regarding the very likely case of what happens if China succeeds in changing the human rights system. As China bonds to the older version of state sovereignty rather than the modern, which is subjected to limitations (Rahman, S., et al. 2022), this boils down to postulating a central question - what could be the impact of China's double-standard diplomacy in the international human rights regime (Rahman, S., et al. 2022)

Conclusion

Human rights laws are respected by many nations under the United Nations Universal Declaration of Human Rights, international human rights laws, and even further specified rights for marginalised groups such as the indigenous community. These legislations protect individuals from facing unjust action against their human rights from other individuals as well as governments. Still, discrimination of human rights can take place within the courts, which emphasises the importance to have such legislations the UN drafts, and countries such as Canada further establish their declaration of human rights for the nation's citizens. This is an ongoing process, and the progression of human rights has improved but there is always room for modification with the increasing awareness of social justice. However, there is difficulty in a common understanding of human rights even with the topic of social justice being so significant and progressive as the debate of cultural relativism and universalists maintains its influence in Non-western nations such as China.

References

Government of Canada. (2023). Canadian Human Rights Act. https://laws-lois.justice.gc.ca/eng/
acts/h-6/page-1.html

Government of Canada. (2023). The Canadian Charter of Rights and Freedoms. https://
www.justice.gc.ca/eng/csj-sjc/rfc-dlc/ccrf-ccdl/

Ishay, M. (2004). What are human rights? Six historical controversies. *Journal of Human Rights*,
3(3), 359–371. doi: 10.1080/1475483042000224897

Rahman, S., & Tan, W. (2022). China's human rights diplomacy and the Uyghur crackdown: the appearance of consistency and the reality of contradiction. China's double standards in human rights. *Trames: A Journal of the Humanities and Social Sciences, 26(1) 35-56.* doi: https://doi.org/10.3176/tr.2022.1.03

United Nations. (2023). Equality and Justice in the Courtroom. https://www.ohchr.org/
en/2014/06/equality-and-justice-courtroom

United Nations. (2023). Human Rights. https://www.un.org/en/global-issues/human-rights

United Nations. (2023). International Human Rights. https://www.ohchr.org/en/instruments-
and-mechanisms/international-human-rights-law

Zhang, Y., & Buzan, B. (2020). China and the global reach of human rights. *The China Quarterly, 241*, 169-190. doi: 10.1017/S0305741019000833

Chapter 9: Human Rights and the Prisons

Ivan Frimpong

Prison Ethics and Human Rights

Prisons have long been a controversial topic when it comes to ethics and human rights. On the one hand, they are designed to protect society by detaining individuals who have committed crimes and keeping them from causing harm to others. On the other hand, prisoners' rights to basic human dignity and fair treatment are often violated, leading to a range of ethical and human rights concerns.

One of the most significant ethical concerns surrounding prisons is the use of solitary confinement. This practice involves separating prisoners from the general population for 22-24 hours a day and is often used as a punishment for misbehaviour or as a means of protection for prisoners deemed to be at risk. However, research has shown that prolonged solitary confinement can have serious psychological consequences, including depression, anxiety, and even hallucinations (Haney, 2018).

Another major issue is the use of force by prison staff. While force may be necessary for certain situations, it should always be used as a last resort and be proportionate to the threat posed by the prisoner. However, reports of excessive force and physical abuse by prison staff are all too standard, leading to serious physical harm to prisoners and a lack of trust in the criminal justice system (Human Rights Watch, 2018).

Furthermore, prisons often lack adequate medical care, leading to serious health problems for prisoners. In some cases, prisoners are denied necessary medical treatment, such as surgery or prescription medications, leading to painful and preventable conditions (American Civil Liberties Union, 2022). This can raise ethical concerns about the state's obligation to provide basic care to those in its custody.

Additionally, the use of prison labour raises questions about exploitation and forced labour. Many prisoners are paid only a few cents an hour for their work, which is often dangerous and physically demanding. Prisons raise various ethical and human rights concerns that must be addressed. From the use of solitary confinement and excessive force to inadequate medical care and the exploitation of prison labour, these issues cannot be ignored. Governments and prison authorities have a responsibility to ensure that prisoners are treated with dignity and respect and that their basic human rights are protected.

Ethical concerns in prisons are the issue of overcrowding. Overcrowding in prisons leads to inhumane living conditions, with prisoners often living in cramped and unsanitary spaces. This overcrowding also makes it difficult for prisoners to access necessary medical care and resources, such as education and rehabilitation programs. In addition to overcrowding, the use of solitary confinement is another major ethical concern in the prison system. The use of solitary confinement has been criticized for its negative impact on prisoners' mental health and well-being. In 2011, the United Nations Special Rapporteur on Torture declared that the use of solitary confinement for more than 15 days constitutes cruel, inhuman, and degrading treatment or punishment.

The prison system is the unequal treatment of prisoners based on race, gender, and socioeconomic status. Studies have shown that racial and ethnic minorities are overrepresented in the prison population and are often subject to more severe punishments and sentences compared to their white counterparts. Women, who make up a growing percentage of the prison population, also face unique challenges, including limited access to reproductive health care and a higher risk of sexual assault.

In light of these ethical concerns, prisons must uphold the human rights of prisoners. The Universal Declaration of Human Rights states that everyone has the right to be treated with dignity and respect, regardless of their criminal history. This includes the right to adequate housing, food, and medical care, as well as the right to education and rehabilitation programs.

The prison system must prioritize the ethical treatment of prisoners and uphold their human rights. The overcrowding and use of solitary confinement, as well as the unequal treatment of prisoners based on race, gender, and socioeconomic status, are all issues that must be addressed to ensure that the prison system is just and fair. Reforming the prison system and ensuring the protection of human rights must be a priority.

This can be achieved through a combination of individual actions and larger policy changes. For example, prison staff can be trained on human rights standards and the proper treatment of prisoners, and conditions in prisons can be improved to ensure the well-being of those who are incarcerated. Additionally, changes to the criminal justice system as a whole can help address the systemic inequalities that exist and ensure that the punishment fits the crime. Overall, the ethics of the prison system must be constantly re-evaluated to ensure that the rights of all individuals are protected. It is only through sustained effort and meaningful action that we can create a prison system that truly serves justice and protects the rights of all individuals.

Treatment of Prisoners

The treatment of prisoners is a topic of great concern to human rights organizations, governments, and the general public. Prisons are designed to protect society from dangerous individuals, but the conditions of incarceration can also cause significant harm to prisoners themselves. In this article, we will examine the treatment of prisoners and the various factors that influence it.

In the United States, the treatment of prisoners is governed by the Eighth Amendment to the Constitution, which prohibits cruel and unusual punishment. Despite this, prisoners often face inhumane conditions, such as overcrowding, lack of access to healthcare, and abuse by staff. In 2011, the U.S. Department of Justice found that nearly 10,000 allegations of staff sexual abuse were reported in American prisons over four years (Human Rights Watch, 2011).

In Europe, the treatment of prisoners is regulated by the European Convention on Human Rights. The European Committee for the Prevention of Torture has found that prisoners in several European countries have been subjected to ill-treatment, including physical violence and solitary confinement.

The treatment of prisoners is influenced by a variety of factors, including the type of crime committed, the sentence length, and the resources available to the prison. For example, individuals convicted of violent crimes may be placed in maximum-security prisons, where conditions are often harsher than in other facilities. Prisons with inadequate resources may be unable to provide necessities, such as food, water, and healthcare.

In addition to the physical conditions of incarceration, prisoners' mental health is also at risk. Solitary confinement, for instance, has been linked to increased rates of depression, anxiety, and suicide. The lack of access to education and job training can also have long-term effects on a prisoner's prospects, making it difficult for them to reintegrate into society upon release.

Despite the challenges faced by prisoners, there are efforts underway to improve the treatment of prisoners and support their rehabilitation. Many countries have implemented programs that provide education, job training, and mental health services to prisoners. These programs have been shown to reduce recidivism and improve outcomes for both prisoners and society as a whole (Nellis, 2016). In many countries, prisoners are subjected to inhumane and degrading conditions, including overcrowding, inadequate healthcare, and physical abuse. This type of treatment is not only inhumane, but it is also counter-productive, as it can lead to further criminal behaviour and a lack of remorse for past actions.

On the other hand, many countries have implemented programs and initiatives aimed at improving the treatment of prisoners. This can include providing education and job training opportunities, access to mental and physical health services, and offering programs for addiction treatment and rehabilitation. These programs have been shown to have a positive impact on the well-being of prisoners and their likelihood of successfully reintegrating into society.

In addition, there is a growing recognition of the importance of rehabilitation and restorative justice in the treatment of prisoners. This approach seeks to repair the harm caused by crime and help prisoners take responsibility for their actions, rather than simply punishing them. Restorative justice programs can include activities such as mediating a conversation between the victim and the offender and engaging in community service.

The treatment of prisoners is a complex issue that requires a multi-faceted approach. It is crucial for governments, policymakers, and society as a whole to recognize the importance of treating prisoners with dignity and respect and to provide them with the resources and support they need to successfully reintegrate into society. By doing so, we can help reduce crime, promote public safety, and create a more just and equitable society. The treatment of prisoners can have a significant impact on their future and the future of society as a whole. While significant challenges exist, there are also opportunities to make positive changes and improve the lives of prisoners. By addressing the factors that influence the treatment of prisoners, we can work towards a more just and humane system of incarceration. We must work to improve the conditions in which prisoners are held and provide them with the resources and support they need to make positive changes in their lives. By doing so, we can help reduce crime, improve public safety, and create a more just and equitable society for all.

Conditions of Detention

Conditions of detention refer to the environment, facilities, and services provided to individuals held in detention, including prisoners, detainees, and immigrants. These conditions play a crucial role in ensuring that individuals' basic human rights are upheld while detained. Poor conditions in detention can lead to a range of negative outcomes, including increased violence, mental health issues, and physical health problems.

One of the key aspects of detention conditions is the physical environment. Overcrowding, inadequate ventilation, and poor sanitation can all contribute to the spread of infectious diseases and the development of health problems among detainees (World Health Organization, 2020). Additionally, poor physical conditions can contribute to mental health issues among detainees, such as anxiety and depression (United Nations, 2020).

Another important factor affecting detention conditions is the availability of basic services. These services include access to medical care, food and water, and hygiene facilities. Lack of access to these services can have serious consequences for detainees, including malnutrition and illness
(Amnesty International, 2019).

In some cases, detainees may also be subjected to physical and emotional abuse by detention staff, which can lead to further physical and mental health problems. Efforts to improve detention conditions are ongoing at the international level. The United Nations Standard Minimum Rules for the Treatment of Prisoners, also known as the Mandela Rules, guide how detention facilities should be managed to ensure the safety and well-being of detainees (United Nations, 2015). The European Convention for the Prevention of Torture and Inhuman or Degrading Treatment or Punishment requires member states to establish independent monitoring bodies to oversee detention facilities (Council of Europe, 2020).

Conditions of detention play a crucial role in ensuring that the basic human rights of individuals held in detention are upheld. Poor conditions can have serious consequences for detainees, including physical and mental health problems, as well as an increased risk of abuse. Efforts to improve detention conditions are ongoing at the international level, with guidance and standards established to promote the well-being of detainees.

The conditions of detention have a significant impact on the health, well-being, and rehabilitation of detainees. Unfortunately, many detention facilities across the world fail to meet the minimum standards required for decent living conditions. One of the primary concerns regarding the conditions of detention is overcrowding. Overcrowding is a widespread problem in many detention facilities, and it is often associated with poor hygiene, lack of privacy, and increased violence. Overcrowding can also lead to the spread of infectious diseases, such as tuberculosis and COVID-19, which can have devastating consequences for detainees, staff, and the wider community. Overcrowding is usually caused by a lack of resources, inadequate planning, or the overuse of pretrial detention.

Another significant concern is the lack of access to medical care. Detainees often have limited access to healthcare services, which can result in untreated illnesses and injuries. In some cases, detainees are denied access to medication or are forced to pay for medical care, which is a violation of their human rights. This lack of access to medical care can also contribute to the spread of infectious diseases, such as HIV/AIDS, hepatitis, and tuberculosis.

The quality of food and water provided to detainees is another critical aspect of the conditions of detention. Many detention facilities serve inadequate or unsafe food and water, which can lead to malnutrition, dehydration, and other health problems. Detainees may also be subjected to long periods of fasting or restricted diets, which can cause physical and mental harm.

Inadequate sanitation and hygiene are also significant concerns in many detention facilities. Poor hygiene can lead to the spread of infectious diseases, such as cholera, dysentery, and typhoid fever. Detainees may also be forced to live in unsanitary conditions, such as overcrowded cells or dormitories with no access to toilets or running water. In some cases, detainees are not allowed to shower or change their clothes, which can lead to skin infections and other health problems.

Finally, the lack of access to education, work, and recreational activities can also harm the well-being and rehabilitation of detainees. Detainees may be denied access to education and vocational training, which can limit their opportunities to reintegrate into society after release. Similarly, the lack of access to work or recreational activities can contribute to feelings of boredom, frustration, and despair, which can exacerbate mental health problems.

In conclusion, the conditions of detention play a critical role in the health, well-being, and rehabilitation of detainees. Overcrowding, lack of access to medical care, poor quality food and water, inadequate sanitation and hygiene, and lack of access to education and work are just some of the issues that need to be addressed to ensure that detention facilities meet minimum standards of human rights and dignity. Governments, policymakers, and civil society must work together to address these issues and ensure that detainees are treated with respect and humanity.

Human rights and prison reform

Human rights and prison reform are two intertwined issues that have garnered significant attention in recent years. The treatment of inmates in prisons has been a contentious topic for a long time, with concerns ranging from poor living conditions to inhumane treatment. Prison reform has become an urgent priority for many countries as they strive to meet international human rights standards. This article will explore the relationship between human rights and prison reform, the obstacles to implementing prison reform, and examples of successful prison reform efforts.

Human rights and prison reform are connected since prisons should uphold and protect the human rights of inmates. International human rights standards, such as the International Covenant on Civil and Political Rights (ICCPR) and the Convention against Torture and Other Cruel, Inhuman, or Degrading Treatment or Punishment (CAT), guide the treatment of prisoners. These conventions specify that prisoners have the right to humane treatment, freedom from torture, and the right to be treated with dignity and respect. The failure of prisons to meet these standards has led to widespread concerns about the human rights of prisoners (OHCHR, 2005).

Prison reform can be a challenging process due to various factors. One of the primary challenges is the lack of political will, which can impede the implementation of reform initiatives. Political leaders may be hesitant to commit resources to prison reform due to the perceived political risks associated with being seen as soft on crime. Additionally, there may be resistance from prison staff who are comfortable with the existing system and are resistant to change. Another challenge is the limited resources available to fund reform initiatives, which may make it difficult to implement significant changes (ACLU, 2022).

Despite the challenges, some countries have successfully implemented prison reform initiatives that have improved the human rights of inmates. For example, Norway has implemented a rehabilitation-focused prison system that has significantly reduced recidivism rates. In this system, prisoners are treated humanely and provided with education and vocational training. Similarly, Germany's prison system has been praised for its focus on rehabilitation, with prisoners given access to education and job training to prepare them for re-entry into society (Petersilia, 2003).

Human rights and prison reform are critical issues that demand significant attention from policymakers, activists, and citizens. The connection between human rights and prisons emphasizes the need to prioritize reform initiatives that prioritize the rights and dignity of inmates. While challenges exist in implementing prison reform, success stories from countries like Norway and Germany demonstrate that it is possible to improve the human rights of prisoners through effective reform efforts. By prioritizing human rights and investing in prison reform, countries can create more just and equitable societies for all.

Human rights and prison reform are complex issues that require thoughtful and comprehensive solutions. The following are some of the key steps that can be taken to address these challenges.

Reducing the use of incarceration is one of the most effective ways to address the issue of human rights and prison reform is to reduce the number of people who are incarcerated. This can be achieved by investing in alternative forms of punishment and rehabilitation, such as community service and restorative justice programs. Improving the conditions within prisons is another important step toward addressing human rights and prison reform. This can be achieved by increasing access to healthcare, education, and job training programs, as well as by reducing the use of solitary confinement.

Increasing transparency and accountability is ensuring that prisons are transparent and accountable is essential for upholding human rights. This can be achieved by implementing measures such as independent inspections and monitoring, as well as by increasing public access to information about prison conditions and practices. Systemic inequalities, such as racism and poverty, are often at the root of many of the issues facing the prison system. Addressing these underlying factors is essential for achieving meaningful reform. This can be achieved through a variety of measures, such as investing in education and social programs, as well as by promoting policies that address structural inequalities.

Finally, involving affected communities in the process of prison reform is essential for ensuring that their voices are heard and their needs are addressed. This can be achieved through community engagement programs and by providing opportunities for formerly incarcerated individuals to participate in the reform process.

Addressing human rights and prison reform is a complex challenge that requires a comprehensive and multi-faceted approach. By reducing the use of incarceration, improving prison conditions, increasing transparency and accountability, addressing systemic inequalities, and involving affected communities, we can work towards a more just and equitable society for all.

References

ACLU. (2022, August 26). *Strategies on reducing reoffending in the United States I. introduction*. Retrieved from American_Civil_Liberties_Union_-_ACLU.UNODC_Submission_Recidivism_Progress.FINAL.pdf

Ashley Nellis, P. D. (2016, June 14). *The Color of Justice: 2016*. The Sentencing Project. Retrieved from https://www.sentencingproject.org/reports/the-color-of-justice-2016-report/ The Color of Justice: 2016 – The Sentencing Project

Council of Europe. (2020). *Full list - treaty office - public.coe.int*. Treaty Office. Retrieved from Full list - Treaty Office (coe. int)

Haney, C. (2018, March). *The psychological effects of solitary confinement: A systematic critique.* Retrieved from https://unlocktheboxcampaign.org/wp-content/uploads/2021/02/Haney-ThePsychologicalEffectsofSolitaryConfinement-ASystematicCritique2018.pdf untitled (unlocktheboxcampaign.org)

Human Right Watch. (2011, February 3). *Mental illness, human rights, and US prisons.* Retrieved from https://www.hrw.org/sites/default/files/related_material/Human%20Rights%20Watch%20Statement%20for%20the%20Record_9_22_09.pdf Human Rights Watch Comments on Prison Rape Standards.pdf (hrw.org)

Human Right Watch. (2018, January 19). *World Report 2018: Rights trends in the United States.* Human Rights Watch. Retrieved from https://www.hrw.org/world-report/2018/country-chapters/united-states World Report 2018: United States | Human Rights Watch (hrw.org)

Liberties Union, A. C. (2022, February 15). *Medical and Mental Health Care.* American Civil Liberties Union. Retrieved from https://www.aclu.org/issues/prisoners-rights/medical-and-mental-health-care Medical and Mental Health Care | American Civil Liberties Union (aclu.org)

OHCHR. (2005). *Office of the United Nations High Commissioner for Human Rights.* Retrieved from 0442572_guide.Exp (ohchr.org)

Petersilia, J. (2003). *When prisoners come home: Parole and prisoner reentry. When Prisoners Come Home: Parole and Prisoner Reentry* | Office of Justice Programs. Retrieved from When Prisoners Come Home: Parole and Prisoner Re-entry | Office of Justice Programs (ojp.gov)

Prominent Egyptian activist Alaa Abdel Fattah was tortured. Amnesty International. (2019, October 10). Retrieved from Egypt: Torture of activist Alaa Abdel Fattah illustrates the use of extreme brutality to crush dissent - Amnesty International

United Nations. (2015). *The United Nations Standard Minimum Rules for the treatment of prisoners.* Retrieved from The United Nations Standard Minimum Rules for the Treatment of Prisoners (unodc.org)

World Health Organization. (2020). *Prisons and health euro.* World Health Organization. Retrieved from Prisons and health EURO (who. int)

Chapter 10: Human Rights and Economic, Social and Cultural Rights

Humna Ali

Introduction

On December 10, 1948, the Universal Declaration of Human Rights conducted a large role in providing large advancements in a declaration all around the globe (Eide & Rosas, 2001). However, human rights and economic, social and cultural rights (ESCR) are two categories of rights recognized by international law (Botlhale, 2021). Human rights are civil and political rights that are universally protected and include the right to life, freedom of speech, religion, and peaceful assembly (Botlhale, 2021). ESCRs are economic, social, and cultural rights that ensure a dignified standard of living and include the right to work, education, health, and an adequate standard of living (Botlhale, 2021). Both types of rights are considered essential for the full enjoyment of human dignity and equality and are protected by international treaties and conventions (Botlhale, 2021). In 1993, 171 states came together at the World Conference for Human Rights and proclaimed that "all human rights are universal, indivisible, interdependent and interrelated" (Eide & Rosas, 2001). However, at the time they came up with the Vienna Declaration and Programme of Actions Agreement which states that social economic and cultural rights will become valued and recognised, as equality needs to be seen throughout diversities (Eide & Rosas, 2001). It was determined that the third generation considered solitary rights, the second generation considered human rights, and the first generation considered civil and political rights (Eide & Rosas, 2001). As Canada is a country that recognizes both human rights and economic, social, and cultural rights (Act, 1982). The Canadian Charter of Rights and Freedoms, which was entrenched in the Canadian Constitution in 1982, guarantees fundamental human rights, such as freedom of expression, equality before the law, and the right to life, liberty, and security of the person (Act, 1982). Universally the majority of people have the right to work, education, health, food, and housing in first-world countries.

Right To Working

The right to work is enshrined in Article 23 of the Universal Declaration of Human Rights, which states that "everyone has the right to work, to free choice of employment, to just and favourable conditions of work and to protection against unemployment" (United Nations, 1948). The right to work is further elaborated on in the International Covenant on Economic, Social and Cultural Rights, which recognizes the right of everyone to the opportunity to gain a living by work which they freely choose or accept (United Nations, 1948). The right to work is an important component of human dignity and is critical for individuals to be able to support themselves and their families and to participate fully in society. However, in many countries, there are significant barriers to employment, such as discrimination, lack of education and skills training, and economic policies that do not prioritise job creation (Clark, 2003). To promote the right to work, governments should work to create an enabling environment for employment, such as through job training programs, labour market policies that support job creation, and measures to eliminate discrimination in the workplace (Loosemore et al., 2022). Additionally, governments should ensure that labour laws and regulations protect workers' rights, including the right to safe and healthy working conditions, and the right to form and join trade unions (Clark, 2003). Governments are responsible for ensuring that individuals have access to employment opportunities and that labour laws and regulations protect workers' rights. Additionally, governments should work to eliminate discrimination in the workplace, such as discrimination based on race, gender, religion, or nationality (Loosemore et al., 2022). The right to work is crucial to achieving sustainable and inclusive economic growth and reducing poverty (Loosemore et al., 2022). When individuals have access to employment opportunities, they can contribute to the economy, support their families, and participate fully in society (Loosemore et al., 2022). The right to work is protected in Canada as a fundamental human right, and it is also recognized under Canadian law (Act, 1982). The Canadian Charter of Rights and Freedoms guarantees the right to life, liberty, and security of the person, which includes the right to work and the freedom to choose one's own profession or trade (Act, 1982). In addition, the Employment Standards Act in each province and territory provides minimum standards for employment, such as minimum wages, working hours, overtime pay, and other conditions of employment (Act, 1982). Therefore, it is important to ensure that this right is protected and promoted for all individuals.

Right to Education

The right to education is a fundamental human right recognized by the Universal Declaration of Human Rights and other international human rights instruments (United Nations, 1948). It affirms that every individual, regardless of their background or circumstances, has the right to receive an education (United Nations, 1948). The right to education includes the right to access quality education that is free, compulsory, and available to all without discrimination (United Nations, 1948). This means that governments must ensure that education is accessible to all, including those from disadvantaged or marginalised communities and with equal opportunities for all students to learn and participate. The right to education also encompasses the right to a broad and diverse education that fosters critical thinking, creativity, and curiosity (Cremin, 2009). Education should be designed to promote the full development of the human personality and prepare individuals to be responsible, active, and engaged citizens (Cremin, 2009). In addition, the right to education includes the right to be taught in a safe and secure environment that is free from violence, bullying, and harassment (Cremin, 2009). Schools should be places where children and young people feel secure and are protected from harm (Cremin, 2009). Overall, the right to education is critical to the fulfilment of other human rights, such as the right to work, the right to health, and the right to participation in political and social life. The right to education is enshrined in Article 26 of the Universal Declaration of Human Rights, which states that "everyone has the right to education" (United Nations, 1948). This right is further elaborated on in the International Covenant on Economic, Social, and Cultural Rights, which recognizes the right of everyone to education and calls on states to provide free, compulsory primary education and to make secondary education available to all (United Nations, 1948).

The right to education includes not only access to education but also the quality of education provided. Education should be designed to promote the full development of the human personality and prepare individuals to be responsible, active, and engaged citizens. It should also be provided in a way that is free from discrimination, with equal opportunities for all students to learn and participate (Roux, 2012). To ensure the right to education, governments must provide accessible and affordable education for all, with particular attention to marginalised and disadvantaged groups (Roux, 2012). This includes ensuring that children from low-income families have access to quality education, as well as ensuring that children with disabilities, children from minority communities, and girls have equal access to education (Roux, 2012). The right to education is also closely linked to other human rights, such as the right to work and the right to participate in political and social life (Roux, 2012). In Canada, education is a fundamental right for all individuals (Act, 1982). The Canadian

Charter of Rights and Freedoms guarantees the right to education, and it is also enshrined in provincial and territorial laws (Act, 1982). Education in Canada is primarily the responsibility of the provinces and territories, and each jurisdiction has its education system (Act, 1982). Generally, education is compulsory up to a certain age, usually until the age of 16 or 18, depending on the province or territory (Act, 1982). Public education in Canada is free for all residents, although there may be some fees for things like textbooks and school supplies (Act, 1982). In addition to public schools, there are also private schools and independent schools that charge tuition fees (Act, 1982). Education is an essential tool for individuals to acquire the skills and knowledge they need to secure employment, contribute to their communities, and participate fully in society.

Right to Health

The right to health is a fundamental human right recognized by the Universal Declaration of Human Rights and other international human rights instruments (United Nations, 1948). The right to health is recognized in Article 25 of the Universal Declaration of Human Rights, which states that "everyone has the right to a standard of living adequate for the health and well-being of himself and of his family" (United Nations, 1948). It affirms that every individual has the right to the highest attainable standard of physical and mental health, without discrimination (United Nations, 1948). The right to health assessment was made for more than 194 where the right to health includes access to quality health care services, including preventive, curative, and rehabilitative care, as well as access to safe and clean water, sanitation, and adequate nutrition (Backman, 2008). It also includes the right to information and education on health-related issues, as well as the right to participate in decision-making processes that affect one's health (Backman, 2008). To ensure the right to health, governments must take steps to provide accessible and affordable healthcare services for all, with particular attention to marginalised and vulnerable groups (Backman, 2008). This includes ensuring that healthcare services are available in rural and remote areas, as well as in urban areas and that healthcare services are provided in a culturally appropriate and sensitive manner (Backman, 2008). The right to health also requires that governments address social determinants of health, such as poverty, inadequate housing, and unsafe working conditions, which can have negative impacts on health outcomes (Backman, 2008).

Governments should also take steps to prevent and control communicable and non-communicable diseases and to promote healthy behaviours and lifestyles (Backman, 2008). Overall, the right to health is critical to the fulfilment of other human rights, such as the right to education and the right to work. A healthy population is essential for individuals to lead productive and fulfilling lives and to fully participate in society (Backman, 2008). In Canada, the right to health is not specifically enshrined in the Constitution, but access to health care is considered a fundamental right (Act, 1982). The Canada Health Act, which was passed in 1984, outlines the principles that guide the country's publicly funded healthcare system, and it ensures that all Canadian citizens and permanent residents have access to medically necessary hospital and physician services (Flood & Thomas, 2016). Under the Canada Health Act, the federal government provides funding to the provinces and territories to support the delivery of health care services (Act, 1982). Each province and territory has its healthcare system, and they are responsible for delivering and managing healthcare services within its jurisdictions (Act, 1982). The publicly funded healthcare system in Canada provides universal access to essential medical services, including doctor visits, hospital stays, and diagnostic tests (Act, 1982). However, there may be some limitations and wait times for non-emergency procedures, and some services, such as dental care and prescription drugs, are not covered by the publicly funded system (Act, 1982). A healthy population is essential for individuals to lead productive and fulfilling lives and to fully participate in society.

Right to Food

The right to food is a fundamental human right recognized by the Universal Declaration of Human Rights and other international human rights instruments (United Nations, 1948). It affirms that every individual has the right to adequate and nutritious food, without discrimination (United Nations, 1948). The right to food includes both physical and economic access to food (Mechlem, 2004). Physical access means that individuals have the means to obtain food, such as through production, purchase, or gift. Economic access means that individuals have the resources to purchase food without compromising their other basic needs (Mechlem, 2004). To ensure the right to food, governments must take steps to provide food security for all, with particular attention to marginalised and vulnerable groups (Mechlem, 2004). This includes ensuring that food is available and accessible, as well as ensuring that food is of adequate quality and nutritional value (Mpinga & Chastonay, 2011). Governments must also address the underlying causes of hunger and malnutrition, such as poverty, inequality, and inadequate social safety nets (Mpinga & Chastonay, 2011). The right to food also requires that governments respect and protect the cultural and social diversity of food systems and dietary practices (Mpinga & Chastonay, 2011). This includes promoting sustainable agriculture and food systems, as well as respecting the rights of indigenous peoples and local communities to their traditional food sources and knowledge (Mpinga & Chastonay, 2011). Overall, the right to food is critical to the fulfilment of other human rights, such as the right to health and the right to work. A well-nourished population is essential for individuals to lead healthy and productive lives and to fully participate in society. The right to food is closely linked to the right to life, as without adequate access to food, people's health and well-being are put at risk (Mpinga & Chastonay, 2011). It is also closely linked to other human rights, such as the right to water, the right to health, the right to education, and the right to work.

To ensure the right to food is realised, states must respect, protect, and fulfil this right (Mpinga & Chastonay, 2011). This includes adopting policies and programs that promote food security and nutrition, ensuring access to land, water, and other resources necessary for food production, and implementing measures to prevent and address hunger and malnutrition (Mpinga & Chastonay, 2011). The right to food is not explicitly recognized as a fundamental right in the Canadian Charter of Rights and Freedoms or in federal or provincial laws (Act, 1982). However, Canada is a signatory to the International Covenant on Economic, Social and Cultural Rights, which recognizes the right to adequate food as a basic human right (Act, 1982). The Canadian government has taken steps to address food insecurity and improve access to healthy food for all Canadians (Act, 1982). For example, the federal government provides funding to community organisations and food banks to support food programs for vulnerable populations (Galloway, 2017). The Nutrition North Canada program also provides subsidies for nutritious food in remote and northern communities (Galloway, 2017).

Right to Housing

The right to housing is a fundamental human right recognized by the United Nations (United Nations, 1948). It refers to the right of every person to have access to a safe, secure, habitable, and affordable home (United Nations, 1948). The right to housing is enshrined in international human rights law, including the Universal Declaration of Human Rights, the International Covenant on Economic, Social and Cultural Rights, and the Convention on the Rights of the Child (United Nations, 1948). The right to housing is closely linked to the right to life, as without adequate access to safe and secure housing, people's health and well-being are put at risk (Hoshmann, 2013). It is also closely linked to other human rights, such as the right to water, the right to sanitation, the right to health, and the right to education (Hoshmann, 2013). To ensure the right to housing is realised, states have an obligation to respect, protect, and fulfil this right (Hoshmann, 2013). This includes adopting policies and programs that promote affordable housing, preventing forced evictions, providing assistance to those who are homeless or at risk of homelessness, and ensuring access to basic services and infrastructure necessary for housing, such as water and sanitation (Hoshmann, 2013). The right to housing is a human right recognized by the United Nations, and it is closely linked to other human rights, such as the right to water, sanitation, health, education, and work (Hoshmann, 2013). The right to housing refers to the right of every person to have access to a safe, secure, habitable, and affordable home, as well as protection from forced eviction and homelessness (Hoshmann, 2013). The right to housing has been recognized as essential for the enjoyment of other human rights, such as the right to health, education, and work. Lack of access to safe and adequate housing can have negative impacts on individuals and communities, such as health problems, reduced economic opportunities, and social exclusion (Hoshmann, 2013).

To ensure the right to housing is realised, governments must take appropriate measures to respect, protect, and fulfil this right (Hoshmann, 2013). This includes adopting policies and programs that promote affordable housing, preventing forced evictions, and providing assistance to those who are homeless or at risk of homelessness (Hoshmann, 2013). In Canada, the right to housing is not explicitly recognized as a fundamental right in the Constitution, but access to safe and affordable housing is considered a basic human right (Act, 1982). The federal government has committed to implementing the right to housing through the National Housing Strategy, which was launched in 2017 (Ramage et al., 2021). The National Housing Strategy aims to reduce homelessness and improve access to affordable housing across the country (Ramage et al, 2021). The strategy includes initiatives such as the Canada Housing Benefit, which provides direct financial assistance to low-income households, and the Rapid Housing Initiative, which funds the construction of new affordable housing units (Ramage et al, 2021). In addition, several provinces and territories have their housing programs and policies aimed at addressing housing affordability and homelessness (Ramage et al, 2021). These initiatives include rent control measures, social housing programs, and support for community organisations working on housing issues (Ramage et al, 2021). Despite these efforts, many Canadians still struggle to find and maintain safe and affordable housing. Homelessness is a significant issue in many communities, particularly among Indigenous peoples and those with mental health and addiction challenges (Ramage et al, 2021). There are ongoing calls for increased investment in affordable housing and more comprehensive policies to address housing insecurity and homelessness in Canada (Ramage et al, 2021).

Conclusion

The discussion made clear as to Human Rights and Economic, Social and Cultural Rights are all essential for humans to survival necessities. Human rights refer to the basic rights and freedoms that are entitled to every individual regardless of their race, gender, nationality, religion, or any other status. These rights include civil and political rights, such as freedom of speech, the right to a fair trial, and the right to vote, as well as economic, social, and cultural rights (United Nations, 1948). However, rights to work, education, health, food, and housing should be required for citizens are essential to the full realisation of human potential and the enjoyment of a life of dignity (United Nations, 1948). Moreover, these rights are closely interconnected, and the enjoyment of one right often depends on the enjoyment of others. For example, the right to education is crucial for the enjoyment of the right to work and the right to an adequate standard of living, while the right to health is essential for the enjoyment of other rights, such as the right to education and the right to work. All rights are connected and without one or other rights can build complexities within an individual life. In summary, human rights are universal, inalienable, and indivisible, and include civil and political rights as well as economic, social, and cultural rights (United Nations, 1948). The enjoyment of these rights is essential to the dignity and worth of every human being, and they are recognized in a range of international human rights instruments
(United Nations, 1948).

References

Act, C. (1982). Part 1: Canadian charter of rights and freedoms. Retrieved from http://tanakiwin.com/wp-system/uploads/2013/10/i-Constitution-Act-1982.pdf

Backman, G., Hunt, P., Khosla, R., Jaramillo-Strouss, C., Fikre, B. M., Rumble, C. & Vladescu, C. (2008). Health systems and the right to health: an assessment of 194 countries. *The Lancet, 372*(9655), 2047-2085. doi: 10.1016/S0140-6736(08)61781-X

Botlhale, E. (2021). The Case for the Constitutionalisation of Economic, Social and Cultural Rights (ESCRs) in Botswana. *African Journal of Legal Studies, 13*(3), 218-243. Retrieved from https://brill.com/view/journals/ajls/13/3/article-p218_3.xml

Clark, L. D. (2003). A civil rights task: Removing barriers to employment of ex-convicts. *USFL Rev., 38*, 193. Retrieved from https://heinonline.org/HOL/Page?handle=hein.journals/usflr38&div=18&g_sent=1&casa_token=R5W1KLXAcIcAAAAA:16RtFmozH4KfRHV_pH58PX9J-1pSpOFulDNrPhodkjCzXRhgOpbFnPzNi-FGpZzme9cPY1M&collection=journals

Cremin, T. (2009). Creative teachers and creative teaching. *Creativity in primary education, 11*(1), 36-46. Retrieved from https://books.google.ca/books?hl=en&lr=&id=FYjX4pYe2X0C&oi=fnd&pg=PT54&dq=diverse+education+that+fosters+critical+thinking,+creativity,+and+curiosity.&ots=PFxdErHA5H&sig=-oO3I-7GNsHOquo7dE4OVKJnb9sY#v=onepage&q&f=false

Eide, A., & Rosas, A. (2001). Economic, social and cultural rights: A universal challenge. In *Economic, social and cultural rights* (pp. 3-7). Brill Nijhoff. Retrieved from https://brill.com/display/book/edcoll/9789047433866/B9789047433866_s005.xml#

Flood, C. M., & Thomas, B. (2016). Modernising the Canada Health Act. *Dalhousie LJ, 39*, 397. Retrieved from https://heinonline.

org/hol-cgi-bin/get_pdf.cgi?handle=hein.journals/dalholwj39&-section=21

Galloway, T. (2017). Canada's northern food subsidy Nutrition North Canada: a comprehensive program evaluation. *International journal of circumpolar health*, *76*(1), 1279451. doi: 10.1080/22423982.2017.1279451

Hohmann, J. (2013). *The right to housing: Law, concepts, possibilities*. Bloomsbury Publishing. Loosemore, M., Alkilani, S. Z., & Hammad, A. W. (2022). Barriers to employment for refugees seeking work in the Australian construction industry: an exploratory study. *Engineering, Construction and Architectural Management*, *29*(2), 619-642. Retrieved from https://books.google.ca/books?hl=en&lr=&id=9YfbBAAAQBAJ&oi=fnd&pg=PR1&dq=right+to+housing&ots=mtV8zlNrhh&sig=LgDKS-4gFoE1A1ZhhA_iizHCZLW4#v=onepage&q=right%20to%20housing&f=false

Loosemore, M., Alkilani, S. Z., & Hammad, A. W. (2022). Barriers to employment for refugees seeking work in the Australian construction industry: an exploratory study. *Engineering, Construction and Architectural Management*, *29*(2), 619-642. doi: 10.1108/ECAM-08-2020-0664

Mechlem, K. (2004). Food Security and the Right to Food in the Discourse of the United Nations. *European Law Journal*, *10*(5), 631-648. Retrieved from **doi: 10.1111/j.1468-0386.2004.00235.x**

Mpinga, E. K., & Chastonay, P. (2011). Satisfaction of patients: a right to health indicator? *Health policy*, *100*(2-3), 144-150. doi: 10.1016/j.healthpol.2010.11.001

Ramage, K., Bell, M., Zaretsky, L., Lee, L., & Milaney, K. (2021). Is the Right to Housing Realized in Canada? Learning from the Experiences of Tenants in Affordable Housing Units in a Large Canadian City. *Societies*, *11*(2), 53. Retrieved from https://www.mdpi.com/1134988

Roux, C. (Ed.). (2012). *Safe Spaces: Human Rights Education in Diverse Diverse* (Vol. 5). Springer Science & Business Media. Retrieved from https://books.google.ca/books?hl=en&lr=&id=P460_vFhtn8C&oi=fnd&pg=PR5&dq=diverse+education+rights&ots=5GvShnOL_n&sig=I-JWf-BO7_9XMalJjG0F6yArdvjc#v=onepage&q=diverse%20education%20rights&f=false

United Nations. (1948). *Universal declaration of human rights*. United Nations. Retrieved from https://www.un.org/en/about-us/universal-declaration-of-human-rights

Chapter 11: Human Rights and Environmental Protection

Janice Wong

Introduction

Every human being depends on our environment to meet our basic needs. The fundamental needs of safe and secure housing, clean water and air, and healthy foods are necessary for life. With such significance and importance, the need to protect the environment is just as important as life itself. The support for environmental protection is not solely a matter of the conservation and preservation of mother nature, but also a necessary measure to ensure the protection of our human rights to a clean and healthy environment. In this chapter, we will examine the different policies that aim to protect our environmental rights, as well as the ethical implications of how these policies are created and the effects they have on our society.

Right to a healthy environment

Under Canada's constitution, "the right to a healthy environment" is not specifically stated under federal law. This human right falls under the *Canadian Environmental Protection Act, 1999* (CEPA) as this law governs the protection of the environment and human health from pollution and toxic substances. Some provincial laws further recognize this right, for example under *Quebec's Environment Quality Act,* it is recognized that a healthy environment is a fundamental human right.

Division of Power

In Canada's constitution, "the environment" is not listed or assigned to a particular level of government. Due to this, it is recognized that certain environmental issues will have both local and national implications and so it is allocated to federal and provincial legislatures depending on the subject matter or the specific environmental issue at hand. However, coordination among various levels of government is needed to effectively establish, manage, and propose laws about the environment. At the federal level, the government is responsible for a wide range of environmental issues. This includes issues such as the management and protection of public property rights, national parks, and other protected areas, as well as the regulation of fisheries, marine and freshwater environmental issues, navigation and shipping, and land rights of Aboriginal peoples. The federal government also has the power to establish national policies that provincial governments adhere to. On the other hand, provincial subject matters are primarily responsible for managing the environment within their borders where they are in charge of setting and enforcing environmental standards, and monitoring and regulating activities. These activities may include mining and lumbering, waste management, recycling, drinking water, and wastewater. Other natural resources such as forests, wildlife, and water are often managed by their respective provinces (Becklumb 2019).

Air, Water, Land

When looking at environmental issues relating to air, we again see the varying levels of government power at play. The provincial government has the most jurisdiction over industries such as mining and manufacturing and therefore is also responsible for monitoring and regulating emissions from these industries. The federal government however is responsible for certain industries such as aviation, and interprovincial and international transportation. Usually, as a result of these industries, toxic substances such as mercury and asbestos are sometimes released into the air, land, and water. Toxic substances are now contained in CEPA meaning it can be considered a criminal offence to release toxic substances, making it a federal responsibility. When monitoring greenhouse gases, greenhouse gas emissions are usually regulated by provinces and territories. They may regulate emissions from specific industries or activities. They may also impose provincial taxes such as the carbon tax, and other regulations that involve property and civil rights, such as emissions trading schemes. This does not mean that the federal government does not have any jurisdiction, recently the *Greenhouse Gas Pollution Pricing Act* was enacted in 2018. This meant that industries across Canada emitting greenhouse gases above a certain threshold were subject to fines (Government of Canada, 2022).

As mentioned before, the federal government is in charge of regulations relating to fisheries, shipping, and navigation. Their jurisdiction over bodies of water do not change whether or not the water is in a lake, river, or stream. These bodies of water are either owned by the federal or provincial Crown or are privately owned. The federal government is in charge of not only regulating fish and fisheries but also fish habitats and other marine animals or plants. This involves the protection of mammals such as whales, walruses, and seals. Alongside this, the federal government is in charge of regulating shipping. This includes monitoring emissions from ships or boats, sewage, or possible oil spills. The courts have recognized the right to navigate waterways, and so regardless of who owns a waterway, vessels of all sizes have the right to navigate any Canadian waterway. When looking at the provincial side, water management is contained within their respective borders. The exception to this rule is when international or interprovincial pollution occurs, in which other parties of government are involved. Territories however are treated differently than provinces. Bodies of water in territories fall entirely under federal jurisdiction, as territories such as Nunavut, are not yet responsible for managing their water resources (Becklum, 2019).

In terms of clean drinking water, Canada typically delegates municipalities for the day-to-day operations of water treatment facilities; however, it is the federal government that imposes the laws and regulations needed for safe and clean drinking water. The exception to this is First Nations reserves, for which the federal government is responsible as these reserves usually include national forests and parks.

When looking at environmental issues relating to land, jurisdiction depends on which level of government owns the land. Rivers and waters are also included in this. The federal government discerns which lands are to be national parks, protected areas, provincial and private land or other wildlife areas. In terms of the wildlife on these lands, in most cases, provinces will have jurisdiction over them if they lie within their respective borders. Some exceptions to this are wildlife on any federal lands such as national parks and other national wildlife areas, as well as certain aquatic species and migratory birds. The federal government is also in charge of monitoring international and interprovincial trades of wildlife through the federal act, *Wild Animal and Plant Protection and Regulation of International and Interprovincial Trade Act* (Becklum, 2019).

The Canadian Environmental Protection Act, 1999

Over the past decades, there have been significant developments in Canadian environmental law. *The Canadian Environmental Protection Act,* of 1999 aims to prevent pollution and protect the environment and human health. CEPA emphasises Canadians' right to live in a healthy place; however, the goal of CEPA is to contribute to sustainable development, meaning that the needs of the present generation should not compromise the needs of future generations (Government of Canada, 2022). The main points that CEPA focuses on are making pollution prevention the foundation of national efforts in combating toxic waste, imposing processes that assess environmental and human health risks caused by pollution, providing tools to manage toxic substances, ensuring the safe disposal of toxic substances, allowing for more effective co-operation with the Canadian government and Aboriginal peoples, and overall continuing to strengthen and reinforce CEPA regulations.

A recent proposal in 2022, aimed to strengthen the CEPA. Bill S-5, originally named *Strengthening Environmental Protection for a Healthier Canada Act* focuses on protecting Canadians' health from harmful chemicals and other toxic pollutants. Bill S-5 would require the development of a new plan for chemical management, as well as a new plan to assess and manage health risks that toxic substances might impose. Bill S-5 also proposes a publicly available Watch List that all citizens and Canadian businesses can have access to, to see which substances they may wish to avoid (Government of Canada, 2022). Overall, Bill S-5 centres around the modernization of CEPA, making its information more accessible and allowing communities such as marginalised groups to gain a better understanding of different harmful substances.

Environmental Indigenous Rights

The Canadian government recognizes that Indigenous people have a unique relationship with the land. As such, Indigenous land rights are protected by Section 35 of the Constitution Act, 1982. Section 35 recognizes the existing aboriginal and treaty rights and provides protection for these rights. These rights include the right to use and occupy land, the right to hunt and fish, and the right to participate in conservation efforts (Constitution Act, 1982, s.35). Historically, Indigenous peoples have been inhabitants of the land for thousands of years and have special and effective methods in managing and preserving the environment. In recent years, the Canadian government has recognized the growing importance of Indigenous culture and knowledge and the need to incorporate this into Canada's own environmental management and conservation efforts. The Canadian government has been building stronger relationships with indigenous communities and has worked together with them in incorporating their perspectives and knowledge into the environmental decision-making process.

Despite the ongoing cooperation between the Canadian government and Indigenous peoples regarding land and environmental protection, there are still many other environmental and non-environmental barriers that Aboriginal communities experience. Many First Nations still don't have access to clean drinking water- a right that is heavily emphasised in Canada's constitution. As of February 2023, around 19% of drinking water advisories are still on reserves (Indigenous and Northern Affairs Canada, 2023). This means that many First Nation communities still don't have access to clean drinking water. The historical relationship between First Nations communities and Canada has been deeply rooted in colonialism, assimilation, and systematic injustice. As part of a marginalised group, the needs of the First Nations have been overlooked by the Canadian government. The environmental injustices of unsafe drinking water highlight the significant ethical gap that exists, as many First Nations continue to suffer today. By considering the ethical implications of economic activities, we can get a better understanding of how environmental degradation disproportionately affects marginalised communities.

Canadian Environmental Protection on a National Level

In 2015, Canada entered a climate change agreement alongside 194 other countries. This agreement is known as the Paris Agreement and aims to fight climate change. The goals set by the agreement are to reduce greenhouse gas emissions by 40% by 2030, with a global goal of reducing global warming to 1.5 degrees Celsius above pre-industrial levels. According to the Climate Action Tracker, as of 2020, Canada is seen experiencing a downward trend (Climate Action Tracker, 2023). Multiple reasons point to Canada's lack of efforts in sticking to its climate policy agenda. In April 2022, Canada approved a huge offshore oil and gas project, and so despite Canada's efforts towards sustainable energy, oil and gas are still primarily used. Canada has stated in the past that they aim to achieve net zero emissions in 2050 but have done little to no action in outlining or proposing policies that help this goal. While some initiatives were introduced over the years, such as carbon taxes, investments in clean energy technology, and support of electric vehicles, significant effort on Canada's behalf is still needed if the Canadian government wants to achieve their climate change goals.

Ethics and Environmental Policies

When looking at ethical environmental perspectives, it's important to look at environmental economics. Environmental economics helps us explain and understand why certain environmental policies and economic activities have the effects they do. Understanding environmental economics allows us to address many human rights issues as it provides tools and models that help us evaluate the costs and benefits of these instated policies, as well as monitor the impacts they have on vulnerable communities. Oftentimes, it's marginalised communities and future generations that suffer from environmental pollution. In Vancouver, Indigenous peoples are most exposed to higher cumulative air pollution, while in Toronto and Montreal, it lies in immigrant residences (Wickramsasinghe, 2020). Pollution can cause respiratory issues and other health problems, affecting mainly low-income communities that live near industrial areas that in turn produce lots of pollution. Another example can be seen among Inuit peoples. Their basic needs of hunting and fishing are in jeopardy as climate change renders certain hunting grounds useless. The overall decline of animals and other natural resources greatly affects these communities as shipping and transporting resources high up north is costly. As we fail to sustain ourselves with natural resources, only those who are wealthy enough will be able to afford these resources at their higher prices, showing just how climate change disproportionately affects people.

Environmental economics also affects the way businesses operate. By using market-based mechanisms such as carbon taxes or cap-and-trade systems, encourages businesses to act more ethically. Environmental economics helps design and promote environmental sustainability and social justice. Overall, because of the huge role that environmental economics plays, we must analyse how environmental policies are created, and the challenges that come with proposing them.

Environmental Economics

Environmental economics is a discipline within economics that deals with the management and utilisation of environmental resources. It's important to touch upon this as environmental economics plays a big part in the creation of environmental policies as the fundamental objective of them is to find a balance between human needs and desires, and the environmental impacts resulting from human activities.

While environmental policies are critical in the role of Canada's sustainable development, it is not easy to instate these policies due to many challenges. One such challenge involves the difficulty in quantifying-term the health risks and pollution that result from environmental degradation. It is difficult to assess the indirect costs associated with treating these health issues or cleaning up pollution as these issues can appear years later. Therefore, the economic benefits of environmental policies are sometimes difficult to discern. This also makes it challenging for entrepreneurs who prioritise profit maximisation to factor the in environmental consequences of their production processes.

Government policies must reflect the interests of the people, but environmental issues are often sensitive in politics. This is because one side may oppose the policies, arguing that there is no evidence that they are effective, or that they may negatively impact the economy. Environmental protection budgets are usually funded through taxpayer money and therefore, environmental policies should reflect taxpayer concerns, meaning that the government has to find a way to increase environmental morale. For these reasons, there are many barriers to proposing environmental legislation, and so the government must devise incentives that encourage producers and consumers to act in an environmentally conscious manner. Environmental degradation is a result of pollution, which indicates a lack of moral consciousness in reducing human impact on the environment. To encourage people to act in a way that benefits the environment, incentives must be used. The balancing act of not inhibiting economic growth while instating environmental policies is one of the most challenging parts of environmental economics. The concept of sustainable development, which emphasises economic growth while protecting the environment, provides a framework for reconciling these seemingly conflicting goals. Some businesses fear that environmental policies will slow down economic growth, and as a result, view these policies as burdensome. However, others argue that the protection of the environment, human welfare, and the ability to sustain future generations should take priority over economic growth. The challenge is to find the optimal level of environmental protection without significantly impeding economic growth. This requires careful consideration of the trade-offs between economic growth and environmental protection.

As mentioned before, incentives are the main driving force behind many if not all policies. Incentives can come in many forms such as time, reputation (corporate social responsibility), guilt, and risk and uncertainty. In the context of environmental policies, incentives are used to encourage individuals and businesses to adopt environmentally-friendly behaviours. One example that you may recognize is the "pay-as-you-throw/go" model (Field & Field, 2021), which charges individuals for the amount of waste they produce. By charging for waste per bag or bin, individuals are incentivized to reduce their waste production, which helps to decrease the overall environmental impact.

The Effectiveness of Environmental Policies

When considering the impact of environmental policies on economic growth, it is important to examine the economy as a whole. Research has shown that environmental policies do not necessarily lead to lower economic growth (Field & Field, 2021). In fact, in some cases, these policies can promote economic growth by spurring innovation and creating new markets and industries for environmentally-friendly products and services. As well, some parties may argue that environmental policies increase unemployment; however, as the environmental industry grows, this allows for more innovation and employment to take place as investments in biotech and other enviro-tech businesses grow.

The effectiveness of environmental policies in mitigating environmental degradation has become a topic of concern among scholars and policymakers. While environmental policies are designed to reduce environmental degradation, they sometimes fail to achieve their intended outcomes due to perverse incentives. Perverse incentives refer to instances when a policy works against its objectives. This phenomenon highlights the importance of evaluating environmental policies to ensure that they are effective in reducing environmental degradation. As an example, the Canadian government recently banned single-use plastics under the *Single-use Plastics Prohibition Regulations, 2022*. The ban was intended to reduce the consumption of single-use plastics, such as plastic bags, cutlery, and other similar products. While the ban has resulted in a shift towards reusable bags, the effectiveness of this policy in reducing environmental degradation is questionable. A consumer must reuse a cotton bag around 7,100 times to negate its harmful environmental impact (Hunt, 2022). Therefore, the best decision a consumer can make is to reuse whatever reusable bag they already have at home. However, not everyone has the habit of bringing their reusable bags each time they go shopping, and as a result, many reusable bags end up in circulation. Instances such as these are why behavioural economics is important when looking at environmental economics. Behavioural economics is an important field of study in this context, as it considers the psychological and perceptual factors that influence individuals' decisions and actions. Therefore, behavioural economics can be used to understand and improve the effectiveness of environmental policies. Moreover, it is essential to ensure that environmental policies are well-designed and evaluated regularly to minimise perverse incentives and ensure that they achieve their intended objectives.

Another factor to consider when looking at the sustainability of economic growth depends on the stage of development that a country is in. According to Guillaume Vandenbroucke and Heting Zhu, in the early stages of a country's development, pollution increases with economic growth. This is because countries in their early stages of development prioritise urban development, human needs, and production. However, as countries become wealthier, they can devote more resources towards environmental protection, leading to a reversal of the trend in pollution (Field & Field, 2021). This phenomenon is explained by the concept of the diminishing returns model, which suggests that investments towards production will only increase up to a certain point. Once a country has reached the industrial economic stage, substantial investments towards production will no longer lead to substantial increases in output, creating opportunities for investment in environmental protection.

Conclusion

By analysing the implementation of environmental policies, we can identify numerous challenges that arise as environmental issues continue to affect vulnerable communities.

The various frameworks and models found within environmental economihelplps us to better understand how to effectively put these policies in place, minimising harm to not only the environment but also to marginalised communities. While the protection of human rights and the environment *should* be a priority for humanity, we see how heavily the economy influences this, as many private businesses often see these policies as burdensome. Through this analysis, it's seen that the crucial role in protecting our environment also ultimately protects our human rights in our present and our future.

References

Becklumb, Penny. (2019, October 29). *Background Paper: Federal Funding for Health Care.* Parliament of Canada. Retrieved from https://lop.parl.ca/staticfiles/PublicWebsite/Home/ResearchPublications/BackgroundPapers/PDF/2018-45-e.pdf

Climate Action Tracker (2023, February 3). *Canada.* Retrieved from https://climateactiontracker.org/countries/canada/

Constitution Act, 1982, Part II: Canadian Charter of Rights and Freedoms, s. 35, being Schedule B to the Canada Act 1982 (UK), 1982, c 11.

Field, B. C., & Field, M. K. (2021). *Environmental economics* (8th ed.). McGraw-Hill.

Government of Canada (2022). The Government *of Canada delivers on its commitment to strengthening the Canadian Environmental Protection Act of 1999*. Government of Canada. Retrieved from https://www.canada.ca/en/environment-climate-change/news/2022/02/government-of-canada-delivers-on-commitment-to-strengthen-the-canadian-environmental-protection-act-1999-and-recognizes-a-right-to-a-healthy-enviro.html

Hunt, Katie. (2022, December 13). *Here's how many times you need to reuse your reusable grocery bags*. CNN. Retrieved from https://www.cnn.com/2022/12/13/world/cotton-tote-vs-plastic-bags-environment-climate-cost-scn/index.html#:~:text=According%20to%20one%20eye%2Dpopping,to%20a%20conventional%20plastic%20bag.

Indigenous and Northern Affairs Canada. (2023, February 6). *Ending long-term drinking water advisories*. Government of Canada; Indigenous and Northern Affairs Canada. Retrieved from https://www.sac-isc.gc.ca/eng/1506514143353/1533317130660

Wickramasinghe, Sachintha. (2020, December 21). *Marginalized groups experience higher cumulative air pollution in Urban Canada*. UBC News. Retrieved from https://news.ubc.ca/2020/12/21/marginalized-groups-experience-higher-cumulative-air-pollution-in-urban-canada/

Chapter 12: Human Rights and Technology

Divya Rohit

Introduction

Humans have always been fascinated with developing technology that contributes to making life easier. Over the past 50 years, technology has gone from cord phones and factory machinery to handheld devices that hold a plethora of information that can be accessed within seconds. Not surprisingly, though, in recent years, humans have been able to make technology that can learn and "think" on its own. With the help of this new technology, menial tasks have been set aside. They have allowed humans to focus on more ambitious issues to feed our curiosity and urge to become more connected virtually. But, being as it may, a significant relief turning our everyday physical tasks into virtual ones, does it not come at a cost? With the entire world being connected and informed, what information is omitted? What information should be omitted but not? These questions get more personal when we look at technology regarding social media, AI, Cybersecurity and governments concerning human rights and privacy. Is our privacy being invaded? Is our data being collected without our knowledge? Or is all of that happening simply because we are not paying attention?

Ethics of Artificial Intelligence

Artificial intelligence, also termed AI, has recently been a hot topic and is considered revolutionary for its extensive capabilities. AI applications are most notable for their unique programming called "machine learning," which allows AI to make decisions and predictions based on the information it has been given. The AI program is "taught" after numerous permutations the expected answer and uses this data in application for other problems. With this ability, AI also has varying degrees of autonomy(Choung et al., 2022), which allow for the possibilities of AI to be endless. However, does the boundlessness of AI go against some ethics we take for granted? And how can we ensure that AI's decisions are ethically and morally correct?

Imagine this: you are an aspiring author experiencing writer's block and have a deadline approaching in a few days. Your boss wants to see what you have written thus far, but you need to have the quality and quantity of work they usually expect from you. You panic and decide to use AI to write your manuscript. Your boss loves the job, and you reap the benefits from work that is not considered your own and continue to use AI. Eventually, your actions come to light, and any work you put out from now on is not taken seriously, and other companies are hesitant to hire you because of your transgressions. This example is how AI can be used unethically and is a typical conversation that institutions such as schools and careers take seriously. Education institutions consider this type of action an academic offence, and other institutions have a similar outlook on the severity of the action.

While a person can use AI unethically, AI can also be programmed to make decisions. Therefore, programmers must ensure that AI can make the most ethical decision whenever possible if put into an ethical or moral dilemma. For example, a classic moral and ethical dilemma posed to humans would be the trolley problem. A trolley's brakes are broken and barreling towards a track split, and you must decide which side the trolley goes to. However, one person is tied down to the tracks on the right side, and five are tied down to the tracks on the other side. Which side would you allow the trolley to go to? There have been contrasting views on approaching this dilemma as humans, but how should AI navigate this given this incident? One idea is to implement ethical guidelines and codes for various usage levels, from the everyday user to classified government information for AI to follow (Hallamaa & Kalliokoski, 2022). With these guidelines in place, it would offer some sense of trust and reliability that, given an ethical dilemma, AI would respond in a way that would align with humans' ethical standards.

So what do some of these ethical guidelines or considerations look like? The IEEE Global Initiative on Ethics of Autonomous and Intelligent Systems has developed documentation outlining ethics for technology for the purpose "...that encourages technologists to prioritize ethical considerations in the creation of such systems (*ETHICALLY ALIGNED DESIGN a Vision for Prioritizing Human Well-Being with Autonomous and Intelligent Systems,* n.d.)." Some of the concerns they look at are Human Rights and that they are not infringed upon, the prioritization of well-being, accountability of the designers and operators, transparency in how the system operates and minimizing the risk of misusing AI (*ETHICALLY ALIGNED DESIGN a Vision for Prioritizing Human Well-Being with Autonomous and Intelligent Systems,* n.d.). The documentation also takes into consideration personal data and controlling the usage of using one's private digital data, the benefit these ethics could have on an economic scale, the legality and how these ethics could affect how laws are enforced, and policies for education and bringing awareness to privacy, human rights and cyber security (*ETHICALLY ALIGNED DESIGN a Vision for Prioritizing Human Well-Being with Autonomous and Intelligent Systems,* n.d.).

These ethical guidelines are built from the morals and ethics philosophers have studied for centuries, loosely called "classical ethics" (*ETHICALLY ALIGNED DESIGN a Vision for Prioritizing Human Well-Being with Autonomous and Intelligent Systems,* n.d.). "This would include utilitarianism, looking at the outcomes and how it can benefit most people. There are also the "well-being metrics," where human safety, health, society and environmental factors are valued over material gain (*ETHICALLY ALIGNED DESIGN a Vision for Prioritizing Human Well-Being with Autonomous and Intelligent Systems*, n.d.). Also, there is the consideration that these technologies are present to aid humanity rather than vice versa.

With the rise of AI, it is vital that if this technology is placed into a scenario that involves them making a crucial decision, they are making the most moral and ethical ones, with human life and well-being being a priority.

Privacy and Data Protection

There has recently been a lot of conversation around AI and AI ethics. However, while humanity tries to implement ethical guidelines into AI, society must maintain its moral standard while controlling sensitive information.

Have you ever spoken with a friend or colleague about a new product or service and then, later that day, received a bunch of advertisements related to that topic? It almost feels like someone is listening in on you and your conversations. This begs the question, how much privacy nowadays do we truly have? While that scenario may seem slightly far-fetched, privacy and data protection have been a point of contention for many considering the world becoming digital.

The need for privacy is a familiar feeling, especially from the government. For example, changing to online banking took some time to get used to, so imagine your personal information being digitally accessible. The reason for this hesitance is the potential for hacking or for this information to be used without your permission by the government. Of course, no one would want to be hacked because their data could be stolen, and people could risk losing their money and even their identity. The issue is with the

Introduction to Ethics and Human Rights 155

government using this information in their data collection of the population to make possible "unethical" decisions.

An example would be using private information to solve crimes without someone's consent. Data from websites such as 23 and me and ancestry.com could be subjected to police use to solve crimes. While this may seem utilitarian, people sign up for these websites to learn more about their genetic information and not to be directly involved in a crime. Even if someone is guilty of a crime and does one of these genetic testing websites, they are entitled to privacy within the website if it is explicitly stated that their genetic information will not be used. An infamous case that sparked this conversation was finding the identity of the Zodiac Killer using genetic genealogy. These types of cases have pushed sites such as 23andMe to make customers' information more secure and private from 3rd parties and government entities. It is explicitly stated now on the 23andMe privacy tab that "We will not release any individual-level personal information to law enforcement unless we are required to do so by court order, subpoena, search warrant or other requests that we determine are legally valid" (23andMe, 2013) as well as "We give you full control to decide how your information is used and with whom it is shared (23andMe, 2013)."

These are just some preventative measures implemented thus far regarding the information you voluntarily give to websites. However, are any guidelines or laws currently in place to protect personal information? Privacy laws from the majority of countries can be traced back to and are the foundation of privacy laws "Organization for Economic Cooperation and Development's (OECD) 1980 Guidelines on the Protection of Privacy and Trans-Border Data Flows of Personal Data (OECD Guidelines)." In addition, there is PIPEDA, Canada's privacy law (Millar, 2006). This law draws from the ten principles: accountability, identifying purposes, consent, limiting collection, limiting use, disclosure and retention, accuracy, safeguards/security, openness, individual access and challenging compliance (Millar, 2006). PIPEDA can be further explained in how the law is applied, what constitutes "personal information," and what information collected can be used for (Office, 2019). Personal information is "any factual or subjective information, recorded or not, about an identifiable individual (Office, 2019)" such as age, ID numbers, and blood type. Examples of what does not constitute Personal Information are "Personal information handled by federal government organizations listed under the Privacy Act, and Provincial or territorial governments and their agents (Office, 2019)."

Taking a step back, it is apparent why Personal Information needs to be regulated to the point where even the government restricts it. However, we use standard websites and social media daily to share information freely, which may not be as protected as we hope. For example, Instagram and Facebook are popular social media applications. To sign up, emails and phone numbers may be required. If someone's password is weak or easily guessable, that person could risk being hacked or accessing other people's information. There is also the risk of social media applications letting third parties access your information. To see how these applications treat your data, look at the terms of conditions and their privacy policy to ensure the level of safety meets your standard. For example, let's look at Meta's privacy policy. Meta owning Instagram and Facebook, we can see what information is collected " and how the information is shared, "When you share and communicate using our Products, you choose the audience for what you share...Public information can be seen by anyone, on or off our Products, including if they don't have an account. This includes your Instagram username; any information you share with a public audience (*Help Center,* 2018)." We can also see what information is collected, "information and content you provide. We collect the content, communications and other information you provide when you use our Products, including when you sign up for an account, create or share content, and message or communicate with others (*Help Center,* 2018)."

Introduction to Ethics and Human Rights   157

Cybersecurity and Human Rights

AI ethics and data security are important topics to remember when dealing with sensitive information. Databases and other sources must have strong security to ensure that while companies have ethical standards, third-party interference is prohibited from accessing sensitive information.

When discussing data privacy, the issue of government usage of personal data was brought up along with the theme of a third-party entity hacking or bypassing firewalls to access personal information. The idea of cyber security and data protection go hand in hand. A robust system in place means more personal data that can be protected. There are different degrees of cyber security, the most prominent being "top secret" information that governments do not make public. Their cybersecurity would be robust to ensure this delicate information is not breached. On a smaller scale, cybersecurity would go down to a person's computer or smartphone being hacked or someone uploading personal information to a website.

Cybersecurity ties into human rights because, in the digital age, it is imperative to ensure that no human rights, such as freedom of expression or religion, are infringed. In light of this, the United Nations developed a special rapporteur for the right to privacy. Its purpose is to protect human rights such as "...identity and beliefs, and their ability to participate in political, economic, social and cultural life (Special Rapporteur on the Right to Privacy, 2015)." This is accomplished by reviewing existing government policies, developing best practices and ensuring that current laws coincide with international human rights obligations (*Special Rapporteur on the Right to Privacy*, 2015). The main areas of interest for the UN would be Mass surveillance, using and retaining personal data, Forensic DNA databases, as mentioned before, and open and big data (*Special Rapporteur on the Right to Privacy*, 2015).

While cybersecurity measures are implemented on an international scale, it is also important that each country has their policies that it can enforce. For example, in Canada, several acts are in place or the works to further strengthen their cybersecurity, such as Bill C-26, *An Act Respecting Cyber Security* (*ARCS*) and *Critical Cyber Systems Protection Act* (CCSPA) which works to amend the *Telecommunications Act* (Public Safety Canada, 2022). In addition, bill C-26 aims to protect Canadians and strengthen securities across several sectors, preparing, preventing and responding to cyber-attacks (Public Safety Canada, 2022).

Human Rights and Internet Governance

AI ethics, data security, and cybersecurity have given humanity an advantage in everyday life. These tasks are because of the internet and our casual access to it.

AI is considered the new technology that could shortly lead and power many menial daily tasks. With this topic, we discussed how AI must develop or be embedded with a guideline of ethics to ensure that when given a job, it can respond in a way that satisfies the human requirement and places the safety and ethics of humans first. With everything, such as menial tasks being digitized, we as humans must ensure that our data is being used ethically and that we know who has access to our information. This ties into our cyber security themes and how it plays a key role in protecting our data from misuse such as government collection or hacking. Here we want to ensure that our rights are not infringed and that we can exercise our rights online. Internet governance touches more on one's right or ability to do so on the internet, ensuring we can freely express our opinion and not be subjected to things like censorship, surveillance, or limited access to information online.

Using the internet has become such an integral part of our day that it is almost only possible to get work done efficiently, making internet access almost essential. This need for internet access has been noticed by the United Nations. They have created a forum outlining his impending need called "Internet Governance Forum 2022," where they assemble principles to "Connect all people to the Internet, including all schools," to ensure no one is excluded from the benefit of this technology. The hope is that anyone can have safe and equitable access to the internet (Nations, 2022).

In light of the UN creating the internet governance forum (IGF), Canada to has made its own IGF which brings together stakeholders and other civilian members to discuss the issues of AI ethics, internet governance and cybersecurity, specifically in Canada (*About - Canadian IGF,* 2021). The report summarizes the priorities that Canadians need to recognize, whether it be internet governance within or outside Canada (*About - Canadian IGF,* 2021).

Human Rights and Access to Technology.

Similar to the argument of making the internet accessible to all so society can deal with dilemmas such as AI ethics, data and cybersecurity, and internet governance, the same idea can be applied to access to technology.

Every day, we can go on our phones or computers and go online to carry out various tasks. Whether to check social media, continue our school research project or meet with coworkers. We always have access to some form of technology, which has granted us access to the internet and a plethora of information. However, as stated before, since the internet is such a critical factor in our lives, people who do not have access to it are severely disadvantaged in everyday tasks. Therefore, as the internet is becoming more accessible, it should follow that technology should too.

Access to technology may be hard to implement internationally, but we already see in done in smaller doses. For example, schools have computer labs or laptops that students can borrow to complete homework or assignments. Companies also have a similar system in which they will give company laptops to people, which ensures employees have the adequate tools to perform the job and allow companies to keep their information secure by giving specific administration permission to certain employees. Technology also presents itself in other functional forms, such as owning a bank card and having an online bank account to seamlessly transfer money or pay bills. In addition, self-ordering kiosks allow customers to order food or use it at airports to help smooth traffic flow for onsite locations. There are also online versions of stores that will enable customers to browse products online and order from the comfort of their homes.

All of these benefits of the internet and access to technology considerably eliminate the inconvenience of not having it in today's society and should be considered on a grander scale.

Conclusion

Here we have discussed many new themes involving human rights. The first is AI and how it is used to do menial tasks that humans no longer want to put their resources in to ensure high efficiency. In allowing AI to do these simple tasks, we must also be wary of external factors that must be considered. For example, will AI be able to make the most ethical decision given its current guidelines and teachings? There are a couple of policies thus far to target how AI reacts and, hopefully, will be built upon further in the future. Another theme that was discussed was data and data privacy. Our personal information is digitized and, therefore, can be used without our consent, tying into cybersecurity and human rights. Better cybersecurity systems mean better protection of our data which means our human rights will not be infringed. For example, we looked at using forensic genealogy to solve crimes, and while that may seem like a great cause, it inherently may not be the best in terms of ethics. Finally, we talked about internet governance and access to technology and how our human rights, such as freedom of expression and identity online, must be protected. For everyone to freely express themselves, obstacles such as censorship must be eliminated, and advantages such as free internet access must be made available. With free internet access comes access to technology, allowing access to the internet.

Overall, in this day and age, where everything is digitized, humans always strive to make life easier. However, to succeed, we must ensure everyone is treated fairly and that human rights and life are not taken for granted.

References

23andMe. (2013). *Privacy and Data Protection - 23andMe*. 23andme.com. Retrieved from https://www.23andme.com/en-ca/privacy/

About - Canadian IGF. (2021). Canadian IGF. Retrieved from https://canadianigf.ca/about-us/

Choung, H., David, P., & Ross, A. (2022). Trust and ethics in AI. *AI & SOCIETY*. Retrieved from https://doi.org/10.1007/s00146-022-01473-4

ETHICALLY ALIGNED DESIGN A Vision for Prioritizing Human Well-being with Autonomous and Intelligent Systems. (n.d.). Retrieved from https://standards.ieee.org/wp-content/uploads/import/documents/other/ead_v2.pdf

Hallamaa, J., & Kalliokoski, T. (2022). AI Ethics as Applied Ethics. *Frontiers in Computer Science, 4*. doi: 10.3389/fcomp.2022.776837

Help Center. (2018). Instagram.com. Retrieved from https://help.instagram.com/155833707900388

Millar, S. A. (2006). Privacy and security: Best practices for global security. *Journal of International Trade Law and Policy, 5*(1), 36–49. doi: 10.1108/14770020680000539

Nations, U. (2022). *Internet Governance Forum 2022 | United Nations*. United Nations; United Nations. Retrieved from https://www.un.org/en/desa/internet-governance-forum-2022

Office. (2019). *PIPEDA in brief - Office of the Privacy Commissioner of Canada*. Priv.gc.ca. Retrieved from https://www.priv.gc.ca/en/privacy-topics/privacy-laws-in-canada/the-personal-information-protection-and-electronic-documents-act-pipeda/pipeda_brief/

Public Safety Canada. (2022, June 14). *Government introduces new legislation to protect Canada's cyber security*. Canada.ca; Government of Canada. Retrieved from https://www.canada.ca/en/public-safety-canada/news/2022/06/government-introduces-new-legislation-to-protect-canadas-cyber-security0.html

Special Rapporteur on the right to privacy. (2015). OHCHR. Retrieved from https://www.ohchr.org/en/special-procedures/sr-privacy#:~:text=Ana%20Brian%20Nougr%C3%A8res%20of%20Uruguay,mandate%20on%201%20August%202021.

Afterword

Ethics and human rights are inextricably linked. Throughout this book, we have discussed, human rights and ethics, their development, and ultimately tangible outcomes that have shaped societal development in modernity. Morality, existentialism, humanity, and related concepts have been discussed. This book has combed the annals of history and human development, but merely provides a precursory introduction to the field of ethics and human rights. We hope that we have not just introduced you to matters pertinent to humanity, but that it has engaged your interest and initiated a passion to learn more.

www.ingramcontent.com/pod-product-compliance
Lightning Source LLC
Chambersburg PA
CBHW030116170426
43198CB00009B/635